W9-BQJ-381

STATUE OF LIBERTY

THE FIRST HUNDRED YEARS

CHRISTIAN BLANCHET
BERTRAND DARD

STATUE OF LIBERTY

THE FIRST HUNDRED YEARS

English language version by

BERNARD A. WEISBERGER

The research for this book was made possible in part by the generous assistance of the American Express Foundation.

AMERICAN HERITAGE

NEW YORK

Distributed by Houghton Mifflin Company • Boston

Contents page:

View of New York Harbor and
the Narrows, from an engraving
published in 1891. *Statue of Liberty
National Monument, New York.*

Preceding pages:

Life magazine cover, January 23,
1908. *Private Collection, Paris.*

Embroidered silk armband,
made about 1878. *Bibliothèque du
Conservatoire National des Arts et
Métiers, Paris.*

Library of Congress Cataloging-in-Publication Data

Blanchet, Christian.
   The Statue of Liberty.

   Translation of: Statue de la Liberté
   Bibliography: p. 187
   1. Statue of Liberty (New York, N.Y.) 2. Statue
of Liberty National Monument (New York, N.Y.)
3. New York (N.Y.)—Buildings, structures, etc.
I. Dard, Bertrand. II. Title.
F128.64.L6B5713 1985   974.7'1   85-9182
ISBN 0-8281-1189-8

Endpapers photograph by Leon Bodycott

C O N T E N T S

Introduction   7

Chapter One
Birth of a Symbol   13

Chapter Two
From Shore to Shore   51

Chapter Three
Toward the New World   77

Chapter Four
The Golden Door   103

Chapter Five
From Memorial to Shrine   129

Chapter Six
The Indelible Image   153

Biography   182

Notes   184

Bibliography   187

Acknowledgments   189

Index   191

A PEEP INTO THE FUTURE.

Its size alone no doubt would have been enough to guarantee the Statue of Liberty large popular affection right from the start in 1886, the year it was completed. Bigger was surely much better in the eyes of most American beholders in that expansive era. When young Theodore Roosevelt of New York, a candidate for mayor the same year, affirmed that big things were in the spirit of the times and a fact of American life, he was addressing a small-town Fourth of July crowd way off in Dakota Territory, but he could have been speaking for almost anybody, anywhere in the country. "Like all Americans, I like big things," he said, "big prairies, big forests, and mountains, big wheat fields, railroads—herds of cattle, too—big factories, steamboats, and everything else."

Frédéric Auguste Bartholdi, the resolute genius of the great work, observed in a letter home, "Everything is big here—even the peas...." As a Frenchman, he preferred his peas small. He also had some difficulty liking Americans, who, by his lights, were deficient in taste and charm. Still, for a land of such expanse he could envision only a statue of "colossal proportions," of "extraordinary proportions."

At the time of completion the statue was not just the largest ever built, but the tallest structure of its kind in the world. A century later the vital statistics still seem fabulous. From its toe to the tip of its upheld torch, the statue is 151 feet tall. Counting the pedestal, it rises 305 feet above the tide. Its head measures 10 feet from ear to ear, its nose a good 4 feet in length. It weighs 450,000 pounds, or 225 tons, its sheathing of hammered copper accounting for nearly half of that. Inside, the route from the top of the pedestal to eye level is a steep climb of 154 steps, the same as a 12-story building. The fact that it stands where it does, taking the winds of New York Harbor full force in all seasons, is testimony to an internal design far more ingenious and important as a feat of structural engineering than most people are aware.

Yet all that hardly explains how we feel about it, our Miss Liberty, or *Liberty Enlightening the World,* as once it was known. For all the statistics, the publicity, for all we think we know about the statue, it remains an extremely elusive subject with many sides and a fascinating history, as Christian Blanchet, Bertrand Dard, and Bernard Weisberger unfold in these pages.

Of utmost importance is the statue's placement, at the gateway to America. It is emphatically a New York landmark. If it had been put up in Washington, D.C., or St. Louis, or anywhere other than New York, we would not feel about it as we do; that is certain. There is simply no better or more appropriate place, which the visionary Bartholdi saw at once, the day he sailed through the Narrows on his initial scouting trip. Indeed, as he later said, his plans for the statue became clear only when he first saw the "thrilling" harbor filled with ships "like a crowd upon a public place."

It was an age that understood the power and value of public places and cared seriously about public monuments and public institutions. New York, largest and wealthiest of our cities, was building them as never before. The fifteen years between Bartholdi's first visit, in 1871, and the unveiling of the statue saw the rise or completion of the Metropolitan Museum of Art, the American Museum of Natural History, Central Park, and the Brooklyn Bridge. Architects and builders and campaigners for funds talked of the civic pride such works engender and how they would "stand down the ages" like the monuments of ancient Egypt. Bartholdi had actually been to Egypt and gazed at "all those marvelous ruins."

In Washington, at the center of Pierre Charles L'Enfant's mall before the Capitol, the Washington Mon-

J udge published this grim view of Liberty's future the week the statue was unveiled. *Judge, October 30, 1886. Private Collection, Paris.*

ument was at last completed (in 1884), the loftiest solid masonry tower ever built. With the colossus in New York Harbor, the nation had two surpassing monuments comparable to those of ancient times.

For Bartholdi, for the workers in the shops of Gaget and Gauthier in Paris who first built, then dismantled and packed the statue for shipment, for Gustave Eiffel, the versatile French engineer who devised its iron skeleton, and for the many thousands of French citizens of all walks who contributed the money to pay for this greatest-ever gift to America, it was both a way of showing French regard for our noble founding principles and of helping the French recover their self-esteem after the debacle of the Franco-Prussian War. Vaunted France, the France of Hugo and Pasteur and Ferdinand de Lesseps, the France of Emperor Napoleon III and what, by reputation, was the most formidable army in Europe, had been crushed by the Germans like an overripe melon. The response of the French people afterward, however, was stunning. They would show that France was France again in "dazzling form," not on the field of battle but in the arts and sciences and with monumental works of peace and progress. Bartholdi himself felt the humiliation of the late war to the depths of his being. He had served in it; he had seen his native Alsace ceded to Bismarck's new Germany.

But it is not simply that the statue, the product of that impulse and that age, stands on or beside the harbor. She is in it, she is of it—on little Bedloe's Island, the site of an old fort and, at odd times, a pesthouse and a gallows. She is surrounded by salt water, by an arm of the Atlantic, which has much to do with how we feel about her. She is thus ever in the midst of passage for all who come and go; alone, unrivaled, her beacon torch visible for miles.

She is like the light left on at home when you go out at night. For all of us who were born here and who have gone away and returned from our travels and from two wars, she has meant just that—"Home, I'm home. This is my place. I didn't take the wrong boat." Coming and going by plane, as we do now, we still pick her out below. "There's the Statue of Liberty! Down there!" you hear people saying with excitement.

For those of us who came from abroad in such overwhelming numbers, year upon year, when Ellis Island was the point of debarkation, she meant welcome to a new home. She marked the threshold. "From her beacon-hand / Glows world-wide welcome," wrote Emma Lazarus in her poem.

In no country other than our own has so much American history transpired as in France and in this century especially, with its terrible world wars. There are sixty thousand American soldiers buried in France, at places with names that are as much a part of our history as are Yorktown or Antietam. For the living who came home, M. Bartholdi's statue had a meaning he never anticipated and that most of us now can only imagine.

I sailed close by her one blustery spring night on an excursion boat with friends. All at once we were directly beneath her. She was brilliantly lighted and brilliantly green and ten times bigger from that angle than I ever imagined, and there was her light blazing high above. We started to cheer.

But what of those others in such different times? Can we ever know what they felt?

"I've never seen anything that looked so good as the Liberty Lady in New York Harbor," wrote thirty-four-year-old Captain Harry S. Truman to his sweetheart Bess Wallace in 1919, on returning from the First World War and the Argonne-Meuse campaign that took more American lives than any other engagement in either war. "You know the men have seen so much and been in so many hard places that it takes something real to give them a thrill, but when the band on that boat played 'Home Sweet Home' there were not very many dry eyes."

We have seen the newsreels from 1919 and 1945 and those expectant faces massed aboard the incoming troopships. We have seen the photographs of immigrants jamming ships' rails for a first look. One of them, Helen Mamikonian, a professor in Boston who arrived from France in the 1950s recalls: "I was a teenager, and I was alone on the boat. It was kind of frightening, you know, to cross the Atlantic by yourself. I met a very nice Italian girl about my age and another Italian, a young boy, and the three of us got up; it was early, five-thirty, six o'clock. We got up and ran to the deck.... She was silhouetted very clear, because we were very close to her as the tugboats came to pull us; we passed her very slowly. Of course we had to look up. She was beautiful.... Imposing, a good word. she looked imposing."

Others of us came to the experience from our own hinterland. Paul Horgan, the distinguished author and historian, remembers as a small boy traveling down from upstate New York with his father, who took him to see the statue because "he was trying to make an American of me." How much is contained in that deceptively simple recollection. And the process continues, with no limit on one's age or sophistication or relative familiarity with American institutions. "I become an American all over again when I see the Statue," remarks Daniel J. Boorstin, the Librarian of Congress, who grew up in Oklahoma.

The statue's appeal as a tourist attraction seems to grow with time. In the past ten years the number of annual visitors has increased seventy percent. It has been glorified, romanticized, trivialized, and over-publicized for purposes that often have little or nothing to do with its intended meaning. Like its near neighbor and contemporary, the Brooklyn Bridge, it has been stitched on pillows, embossed on silver spoons, printed on dinner plates, bandanas, T-shirts, and cocktail napkins. You can buy it in the form of a rubber stamp. And in ersatz bronze, with or without thermometer, it remains the all-time perfect cheap souvenir of New York—the Empire State Building its only rival.

Its image has been enlisted to sell war bonds, biscuits, horsehair brushes, life insurance, credit cards, mineral oil, champagne, cheese, cigarettes, and sewing machines. It has been cartooned and lampooned without end. In this its centennial season, it is being praised and celebrated and photographed as it has not since the damp day in October 1886 when Bartholdi, a marvel in full dress, climbed to its crown to cut loose its veil with his own hand.

Like all great events in history, it needs to be seen in the context of its times, of politics and technology and such largely forgotten and fascinating influences as those of the Freemasons. Like all great achievements in history, it is to a large extent the way it is because a particular group of people were the way they were. It is, among other things, a monument to several glory-struck, gloriously outsized egos of a kind only the nineteenth century could produce, sculptor Bartholdi being the prime example. He is the sort of character Jules Verne might have invented. Imagine discussing with a few friends, over dinner one evening at a country home near Paris, that you want to commemorate America's democracy in some way, a fairly vague discussion that will one day result in the creation of the greatest statue on earth, a structure taller than any ever attempted before, in a distant land where you have never set foot and know no one, and then pursuing that vision with boundless persistence and enthusiasm for the next twenty years!

Besides Bartholdi there is Edouard de Laboulaye, French professor of law and author of a three-volume history of the United States, who was host that evening near Paris, and a participant in the discussion of plans to create a monument celebrating liberty; and Eiffel, who ranks with such giants of heroic nineteenth-century engineering as Brunel and the Roeblings, and whose subsequent triumph, the Eiffel Tower, would become for Paris what the Washington Monument is for our capital.

The Americans include President Grover Cleveland; the brilliant Richard Morris Hunt, the first American trained at the Ecole des Beaux-Arts, architect to the Vanderbilts and Astors and designer of the statue's pedestal; and Joseph Pulitzer, a Hungarian immigrant, the strange, ambitious publisher of the New York *World* who with the power of his paper raised one hundred thousand dollars to pay for the pedestal.

"Colossal statuary does not consist simply in making an enormous statue," Bartholdi insisted. "It ought to produce an emotion in the breast of the spectator, not because of its volume but because its size is in keeping with the idea it interprets...."

The aged Victor Hugo, after seeing the statue in Paris, is said to have written to Bartholdi: "Form...is nothing without the spirit; with the idea it is everything."

The idea, of course, is liberty, and liberty is what we Americans have always wanted first of all. It was what the Revolution was fought for, what the country was founded for. "Hail, Liberty!" was the cry on the day the statue was unveiled. Gilmore's band struck up *America*—"My country, 'tis of thee, Sweet land of liberty..." "We will not forget that Liberty has here made her home," said President Cleveland.

The idea is still everything. The statue is still there, unrivaled at the gateway. She isn't a warrior. She isn't bombastic or threatening. She isn't a symbol of power. The Statue of Liberty is an act of faith.

CHAPTER ONE
BIRTH OF A SYMBOL

On the afternoon of November 29, 1884, a carriage squeezed its way through the crowd of Parisians gathered before the workshop of Gaget, Gauthier and Company, on the rue de Chazelles. There were few secrets in the streets of Paris, and the throng knew the occupant of the carriage was Victor Hugo, the first citizen of the city. He had come to view a monumental piece of copper statuary bearing the impressive title "Liberty Enlightening the World," to be shipped as a present from France to its sister republic, America. It was a fit meeting, for Hugo himself was also an outsized icon of liberty. France's greatest living novelist and poet, Hugo was a revolutionary who had inspired an entire generation of French democrats as they did battle with the monarchists. Now in his eighties, with white hair and beard, dressed in a gentleman's frock coat, Hugo was still a legendary figure of French libertarianism. The cries of "Vive Hugo" and "Vive la République," which followed him wherever he went, meant the same thing.

Hugo emerged from his carriage and went inside to meet the monument's creator, Frédéric Auguste Bartholdi. The two shook hands, and Bartholdi gave Hugo a memento of his visit. Looking up at the statue, which towered to 151 feet, Hugo began to speak. His voice quavered, but it retained the spirit that had called so many Frenchmen to so many battles: "The vast, restless sea now witnesses the union of two great, tranquil lands. This beautiful work encourages what I have always loved—peace. Between America and France—France, which is Europe—may this pledge of peace be permanent."

The idea of offering this extraordinary gift from the French to the American people took root in the minds of a handful of French republicans at a fashionable dinner party at an estate near Versailles in 1865. Perhaps fired by wine, these staunch egalitarians envisioned a monument that would rival the Seven Wonders of the ancient world. Its construction would utilize the latest innovations of the new technology and affirm the superiority of the machine age. It would be a testament to the glory of industrialism triumphant. And, just as loudly, it would proclaim the supremacy of republican ideals.

As their vision grew, they began to see a statue of a great lady symbolizing the American dream. Like all symbols, she would be subject to varying interpretations. The millions of European immigrants who poured through her "Golden Door" made her the symbol of the promise America held out for the less fortunate of the Continent. Native-born Americans made her the symbol of the enduring stability of the nation. In the following century she would be lampooned, ridiculed, appropriated as a political symbol for the far left and right in American politics, and transformed by Communist propaganda into an international symbol of international oppression. She would be used in cartoons, musical comedies, motion pictures, and advertising campaigns. She is the STATUE OF LIBERTY.

The Statue of Liberty, an eternal symbol of hope, was born out of the despair of two of the most devastating conflicts of the mid-nineteenth century: the American Civil War and the Franco-Prussian War. By 1870 America had begun to bind up its wounds from a war that had left more than 600,000 men dead. There was a great explosion of creativity in America, whose engineering marvels and inventiveness had fired a new age of commercial progress. It was a jubilant time for the nation, which had emerged stronger than

On the preceding two pages:

Liberty as she appeared in 1983 against the New York skyline. Restoration work began in 1984. *François Halard, Paris.*

Opposite:

Three men at the foot of the giant statue. *A photograph from the Musée National des Techniques, Paris.*

ever from its Civil War and was looking forward to its hundredth birthday only six years in the future.

But for the French, 1870 was a time of bitter tragedy. Emperor Napoleon III had allowed himself to be lured into a war with Prussia over an attempt to place Leopold of Hohenzollern on the Spanish throne. Napoleon, who had inherited all of the vanity of his famous namesake but none of his skill, personally took command of the French army but was unable to get it across the Rhine. Less than a month after the opening of the hostilities, Napoleon and 83,000 of his men were captured in the rout at Sedan.

When news of the crushing defeat reached Paris, a group of dissident antimonarchists took control of the government and announced the "restoration" of the French Republic. They set up a provisional administration that tried to carry on the fight, but the Prussian army was invincible. The Germans besieged Paris and starved the city into submission. On January 28, 1871, France was forced to sign a humiliating armistice in which Alsace and part of Lorraine were ceded to Germany along with an indemnity of five billion francs.

With Napoleon in exile, no one in Paris was sure what would follow, or whether the new Republic could survive. Napoleon's Empire had been founded in 1852, and was France's ninth major governmental change in the sixty-three years since the Revolution. There had been a constitutional monarchy, a First Republic, a Directory, a Consulate, a first Napoleonic Empire, two more monarchies under different royal families, and the Second Republic, which Napoleon III had overthrown. Each change had been marked by bloodshed as violent political, regional, religious, and class antagonisms racked the country.

Certain groups of Parisians, furious over the terms of the surrender, allied themselves with socialist factions to provoke an insurrection against the Republic. They set up an independent "Paris Commune," the first revolutionary "proletarian" government. The republican members of the provisional government, headquartered in Versailles, would not tolerate what they saw as the tyranny of urban radicals in Paris. They sent in troops and, after bitter fighting, regained control. While the Prussian occupiers looked on, French soldiers shot 30,000 French workers at the barricades in a single bloody week of fighting.

Republican France was bleeding to death. The government called for elections to create an assembly that would write a new constitution for a new and permanent government. It was not at all certain whether the Republic would be scrapped and another monarchy or empire established. If the Republic should survive, no one knew what factions would dominate it.

France's moderate republicans geared up for a hard battle on the field of public opinion. They had been prepared for it by the eighteen years of Napoleon III's dictatorship. Napoleon's secret police had diligently harassed and censored possible opponents of every kind. But the more they did so, the more ardently the republicans clung to their convictions. One of the strongest of those beliefs was that the idea of a republican form of government had been proven by the success of the United States of America.

No one clung to this belief more tightly than Edouard-René Lefebvre de Laboulaye, holder of the Chair of Comparative Law at the Collège de France, and a dedicated liberal. Like his brilliant fellow Frenchman, Alexis de Tocqueville, who had written a penetrating analysis of American manners and institutions, Laboulaye was fascinated by the United States. His many published works included a history of America, a study of the American Constitution, and translations of works by Benjamin Franklin and the New England abolitionist William Ellery Channing.

Laboulaye used his professorial chair as a political pulpit, and in the 1860s liberal students flocked to his courses to hear his barely disguised criticisms of the Napoleonic yoke, which, to escape the scissors of "Madame Anastasie" (the French name for the censor), often took the form of intense praise for the libertarian institutions of America.

At the root of these pro-American feelings was the fact that France had served as midwife to the American Revolution. As Laboulaye never ceased to remind readers, the Marquis de Lafayette had fought at Washington's side and a French army, under General Jean-Baptiste de Rochambeau, had helped win the final victory of 1781. In turn, Americans such as Franklin and Thomas Jefferson had found a spiritual home in Paris, where they had served as ambassadors. Finally France, having helped to plant liberty in America, had followed the American example in 1789 by undertaking a revolution of its own.

Man and the statue. This scale drawing was included in an 1883 fund-raising booklet to inspire awe and generosity in prospective donors. *Private Collection, Paris.*

Edouard-René Lefebvre de Laboulaye. Terra-cotta bust by Bartholdi, 1866. *Collection of Michel de Laboulaye, Paris.*

During America's Civil War, Laboulaye had ardently defended the cause of the Union, especially after President Lincoln signed the Emancipation Proclamation in 1862, thereby removing a long-standing taint of slavery from America's image. Liberals in France found another reason to detest Napoleon III when the Emperor took a pro-Confederate stance. Laboulaye seized every opportunity to convince his American friends that Napoleon's views were rejected by many Frenchmen.

The liberal intelligentsia of Paris were shocked by the assassination of President Lincoln in 1865. A group around Laboulaye got the idea of striking a gold medal in the great man's memory and offering it to his widow. They sponsored a public subscription drive to which more than 40,000 Frenchmen contributed, proclaiming their sympathy for the liberty-loving ideal of Lincoln.

Napoleon got wind of the subscription and ordered all of the money confiscated. But the sponsors had the last word. They gathered up enough cash to have the medal struck in Switzerland and smuggled to Mrs. Lincoln in a diplomatic pouch. This was not simply a tweak of the nose of the Empire. It was an act of faith. On the medal's face, surrounding a profile bust of Lincoln, were the words: "Dedicated by the French Democracy to Lincoln, twice elected President of the United States." On the obverse, along with a replica of the U.S. Great Seal, the medal read: "Lincoln, an honest man; abolished slavery, saved the republic, and was assassinated on the 15th of April, 1865," and "Liberty, Equality, Fraternity!" An accompanying note said, "Tell Mrs. Lincoln that in this little box is the heart of France."

The citizens of Caen sent a letter noting that America's sorrow was shared by "all good men" because Lincoln had met his tasks and overcome them "without veiling the statue [*sic*] of Liberty."

Laboulaye continued to sound the praises of America. Now that human bondage no longer overshadowed the Declaration of Independence, America was a nation faithful to its highest commitments. It was advancing toward its centennial with a confident step. And what an anniversary for poor France to envy. Its "sister republic" had freedom and stability, two qualities in desperately short supply in France.

Laboulaye wanted France to share in America's anniversary. It was a theme he often expounded to the friends—republicans, intellectuals, politicians, academics, writers, and artists—he brought together for dinners at Glatigny, his estate near Versailles. One night in 1865 he proposed the idea of creating something far more ambitious than a medal to the memory of Lincoln: a monument to the American independence for which France had fought. What could be a better sign of where France's heart continued to lie?

Those around the table included the successful and popular young Alsatian sculptor Auguste Bartholdi. Based on his own statements later, it is safe to say that no one listened more attentively.

The turbulence of French politics gave Laboulaye new reasons for his desire to tighten the bonds between his native France and his sentimentally adopted America. If French republicans did manage to keep control of the government, they would benefit by having a strong ally and model abroad. Additionally, the forces of republicanism were struggling against widely disparate political factions, which were calling for everything from a return to the autocracy of Napoleon to radical anarchy. To Laboulaye, the American experience proved there was a middle way.

In 1871, Franco-American relations were far from warm. During the Prussian war, America had been shockingly indifferent. The most it had done was to send some provisions during the siege of Paris. Americans were somewhat distrustful of France's turbulence and many of them, sharing a penchant for order and discipline, preferred to cultivate the friendship of autocratic but stable governments such as those of England or the new German empire.

Laboulaye's first objective was to rekindle warm Franco-American feelings. With the mind of a modern-day public relations expert, the professor seized on the idea of a spectacular demonstration linked to the centennial of American independence, soon to be celebrated with a grand exposition in Philadelphia.

Laboulaye and his friends began to revive his old idea of an American birthday present. A monument, with a double meaning. It would commemorate the completion of a hundred years of American freedom, but it would also celebrate Franco-American friendship and the common values of both republics.

The monument would be called *Liberty Enlightening the World*. Its form was not yet clear in 1871, but certainly it would be something out of the ordinary. A crucial element was the choice of the man who now

Libertas Americana. The terracotta medallion opposite, sculpted during the American Revolution, illustrates an allegory of Franco-American friendship devised by Benjamin Franklin. America is represented by the infant Hercules, shown in his cradle strangling two snakes. France appears as Minerva with a helmet and lance, her dress marked with several fleurs-de-lis. The cheetah symbolizes Great Britain. *Musée National de la Coopération franco-américaine, Blérancourt.*

joined Laboulaye in planning to execute the memorial. It was Bartholdi, and because of him, Liberty would take the shape of a gigantic statue.

In many ways, Bartholdi was a remarkable person, almost as out of the ordinary as the statue itself. And what was most curious was the fact that he seemed artistically unremarkable and lacking in originality. He was a contemporary of the great French masters of painting and sculpture—Degas, Rodin, Cézanne, Manet, and others who were breaking new ground in subject matter, color, form, and the use of light. Yet he was indifferent, if not hostile, to such experiments, and while innovative artists were struggling for acceptance, Bartholdi became the prototype of the artist blessed by official favor.

Opposite:

The **Emancipation of Slaves** by Pezzicar drew admiring crowds at the Centennial Exposition in Philadelphia a decade after the close of the Civil War. *L'Illustration, August 19, 1876. Bibliothèque Forney, Paris.*

The **Liberty Bell.** Engraving by Thomas Nast. *Harper's Weekly, June 27, 1885. American Library in Paris.*

He was born in Colmar, in the province of Alsace, in 1834, to a prosperous middle-class family which, up to then, had produced businessmen, judges, and other professionals, but no artists. His father died when he was young, leaving him in the care of an adoring but powerful and pushy mother, whom he worshiped throughout his life. As a young man he showed a talent for drawing, and was enrolled as a pupil of the painter Ary Scheffer, a friend of the family, more noted for his zealous republicanism than for

Liberty Guiding the People. A detail of Eugène Delacroix's 1830 painting. *Musée du Louvre, Paris.*

American Independence. Engraving by L. Roger after Duplessis-Berteaux, 1786. *Musée National de la Coopération franco-américaine, Blérancourt.*

Opposite:

The Republic Enlightening the World, attributed to A. L. Janet-Lange, 1848. Under the royal government, the work was titled "France Enlightening the World." *Musée Carnavalet, Paris.*

INDÉPENDANCE DES ÉTATS-UNIS.

Le 4 Juillet 1776, les Treize Colonies Confédérées (connues depuis sous le nom d'Etats-Unis) sont déclarées, par le Congrès, libres et indépendantes. N. Gerard, porteur des pouvoirs de LOUIS XVI, Roi de France, Benjamin Franklin, pour les États-Unis, signent à Paris, le 6 Février 1777, un Traité d'amitié et de commerce, et un Traité d'alliance éventuelle, mis en vigueur par la déclaration de guerre survenue entre la France et l'Angleterre.

Le Comte d'Estaing, le Marquis de la Fayette, le Comte de Rochambeau, &c. combattent pour la cause des Américains, soutenue avec tant de gloire par le Général Washington. Capitulation faite le 19 Octobre 1782 par le Lord Cornwalis, dont le désastre accélère la Paix. L'indépendance des États-Unis est reconnue par les Traités de Paix. Pénétrés de reconnoissance pour les services que LOUIS XVI leur a rendus, les États-Unis ont depuis fait élever à Philadelphie un monument qui en éternisera le souvenir. Cet exemple est d'autant plus mémorable, que les siècles passés n'offrent aucun exemple de monumens élevés par des Républiques à la gloire d'un Souvrain. Les Traités de Paix ont rendu aux Nations la liberté des mers; bienfait dont l'Europe est redevable à la générosité de LOUIS XVI. Le Port de Cherbourg, ouvrage immortel du règne de ce grand Prince, doit affermir cette liberté si utile aux Peuples.

A Paris chez Blin, Imprimeur en Taille-Douce, Place Maubert, N.º 17, vis-à-vis la rue des 3 Portes. A.P.D.R.

The bridge at Garabit designed by Gustave Eiffel. *Le Journal Illustré, November 18, 1883. Bibliothèque Forney, Paris.*

The bridge's magnificent central arch, from a contemporary postcard. *Private Collection, Paris.*

anything unconventional in his sentimental canvases. When Bartholdi became interested in sculpture, he worked with Antoine Etex, who had done some of the bas-reliefs for the Arc de Triomphe in Paris, and Jean-François Soitoux, also a very careful, academic sculptor.

But Bartholdi had one special drive. From the start he showed an interest in large-scale works designed for outdoor public spaces. When he was only nineteen, the city of Colmar commissioned him to do a twelve-foot-high statue of General Jean Rapp, a Colmar native who had become an aide-de-camp to Napoleon. Family connections may have helped Bartholdi to land the assignment, but the work was widely acclaimed, and launched him on a career as a much honored creator of public monuments. In time he would do many other memorial statues, including one of Admiral Jean Bruat in Colmar, another of Lafayette in New York, and most notably a memorial to the defenders of the French city of Belfort during the Franco-Prussian War. That one was a huge lion, roaring defiance, carved at the base of a cliff.

In all these works, Bartholdi adhered to principles that he developed early. Since official statues had a pedagogical function, they must express themselves like a good lecture, with simple sentences and striking words without any superfluous ornamentation. He explained it to a reporter for the New York *World* in 1878: "I have a horror of all frippery of detail in sculpture. The forms and effects of that art should be broad, massive and simple. In my 'Lion of Belfort,' since you press me for an example, I have given only the grand outlines. I have not wasted my time in grooming the mane; I have sought only such a distribution of masses of light and shade as may be likely to tell at the distance from which the thing is to be viewed. So far as the Statue of Liberty goes, I can only tell you that I modeled it in accordance with these principles, keeping constantly in mind the 'feel' of the location it was to occupy, and therefore not wasting the force of the work in frivolous details."

All of Bartholdi can be summed up in that credo. He thought in large-scale terms, both for his work and for himself. His admiration for heroic-sized creations was deeply reinforced when, in 1856, he toured

Egypt and was profoundly impressed by its enormous ruins—the Sphinx, the Pyramids, and the huge statues of animal gods that peopled the ancient temples. He called these figures "granite beings of imperturbable majesty, whose benevolent and impassive gaze seems to despise the present and to be fixed on the limitless future." Full of admiration at the way Egyptian craftsmen had mastered the techniques of colossal sculpture, he dreamed of designing similar projects that would guarantee him fame.

But commissions for monuments are rare, and Bartholdi had to make a career and a livelihood doing what sold best at the time—busts of notables. He settled in Paris where he became a successful and conventional society sculptor. In 1865, Bartholdi was commissioned to sculpt a bust of Laboulaye; the assignment led to frequent visits to Glatigny and the professor's circle of liberal thinkers, and eventually to the famous dinner party at which the discussion turned to a project for strengthening the traditional links between French and American republicans.

Bartholdi later claimed that the discussion that night was not specifically political, but dealt only in general terms with gratitude and friendship between nations. Be that as it may, the table talk resulted in Bartholdi's offer to build a monument to United States independence, and it was also agreed that the memorial, being republican in character, should be the result of a joint effort of the ordinary citizens of both countries.

Like many speculative projects born during social conversation, the idea appeared to go nowhere. There would be a period of dormancy, during which other events influenced its final form.

First of all, in 1867, Bartholdi's dream of doing something colossal in the style of the East already seemed on the verge of coming true. He had been reading in the press about the Khedive of Egypt, Ismail Pasha, who struck him as the contemporary reincarnation of the ancient pharaohs. The reason was that in Ismail Pasha's country, and under his instigation, a Frenchman, Ferdinand de Lesseps, was supervising the excavation of the Suez Canal—a work on the mighty scale of ancient Egyptian art.

Bartholdi was fascinated. And when Ismail Pasha visited Paris for the opening of the Universal Exposition of that year, the sculptor—probably at the suggestion of the Empress Eugénie—submitted a plan to him for an immense lighthouse that would stand at the entry to the canal. Celebrating the union of Occidental civilization with the wealth of the Orient—and magisterially joining the colossal, the functional, and the symbolic—Bartholdi's design called for a robed woman holding aloft a torch. It would be called "Egypt (or Progress) Bringing the Light to Asia."

Ismail Pasha accepted the idea, and Bartholdi believed that he had found the kind of wealthy patron who would help him bring a grandiose dream into being. For two years he poured out drawings and models, and even sketched out an idea for a colossal statue of Ismail Pasha to be put on his tomb.

But 1869 brought nothing but disappointment. The Empress Eugénie did formally open the Suez Canal, and Bartholdi, among the guests who were assembled for the ceremony, presented the fruits of his labors to the Egyptian ruler. However, by that time Bartholdi had learned, partly through the warnings of de Lesseps, that Ismail Pasha, whatever he said, was financially incapable of paying for this new wonder of the world. In fact, he was far from a modern pharaoh. His country would soon become an Anglo-French protectorate. Bartholdi sadly packed his visionary Oriental projects into storage boxes.

Although Bartholdi would build no gigantic statue in Egypt, the aborted undertaking was not a fatal blow to his future. He was living in an era when governments began to crave grand memorials to their growing industrial power. The times were right for Bartholdi's old-fashioned ideas.

The last half of the nineteenth century witnessed the triumph of technology, and with it came new opportunities for monumental public creations. The new technology made it possible to create objects that were both functional and visionary—to build structures that were useful but could also dazzle the imagination, if only by their scale, as surely as the decorative arts had delighted the century before. This was particularly evident in the fields of transportation and communication, which attracted large capital and high talent because they had to be improved and perfected to spur industrial and commercial growth. Every major modern country, for example, worked hard to develop a railway network, and out of these networks came such engineering wonders as the viaduct of Garabit in France, which spanned 544 feet with a single arch and was recognized as a masterpiece of metallic architecture.[1] Architects began to design and build bridges of a length once thought impossible. The most majestic of these creations was the Brooklyn Bridge, opened in 1883, stretching a full mile and two-tenths between the busy shores of Brooklyn and New York City.[2] Americans welcomed it as part of a general outpouring of engineering marvels that brought peoples and regions closer together. In 1866 they cheered the completion of the Atlantic Cable. In 1869, the same year that the Suez Canal opened a gigantic shortcut between Europe and Asia, the United States celebrated the completion of the first railroad line that made it possible to go from coast to coast by steam power in a matter of days instead of months.

It was a busy, bustling time for the industrialized nations, and the artifacts of technology brought with them a new kind of imperialism. With their factories booming, the world's major powers looked outward

for markets and raw materials. And with superior military technology and swift transportation available to them, they found what they were looking for in the virtually defenseless continents of Asia and Africa. While the United States beat down the last Indian resistance in the Far West, European nations, especially France, Great Britain, and Germany, seized colonies and established spheres of influence in Africa, Indochina, and China. The age of imperial growth and the quickening pace of transportation supported each other. The Suez Canal was scarcely opened before there was talk of joining the Atlantic and Pacific oceans by a canal through Central America.

It was a golden age of iron, of rugged individuals, including creative engineers such as Gustave Eiffel, who built the viaduct at Garabit; like Ferdinand de Lesseps; like John and Washington Roebling, father and son, who spun the Brooklyn Bridge over the East River. For Bartholdi, it was exactly the kind of age that might, under the right conditions, be hospitable to the idea of statues bigger than anything ever done before in human history, works of art requiring refined mechanical skills for their creation.

During these last years of the nineteenth century, leading nations all held world's fairs as showcases of their industrial achievements. Exhibition buildings rose up to become palaces of progress that housed the most up-to-date machines, the most glittering displays of technical achievement, the latest examples of anything noteworthy in the arts and sciences. Dignitaries and crowned heads came to give official blessing

The Universal Exposition in Paris: The Palace of Nations on the Champ de Mars. *Les Merveilles de L'Exposition, 1878. Private Collection, Paris.*

The Republic. Statue by the Morice brothers, erected in Paris, July 14, 1883. *Bibliothèque Forney, Paris.*

Resistance. Statue by M. Cabet, erected in Dijon, France, 1876. *L'Illustration, July 1, 1876. Bibliothèque Forney, Paris.*

Youth. Statue by M. Chapu, 1876. *L'Illustration, August 19, 1876. Bibliothèque Forney, Paris.*

Opposite:

Germania. Statue by J. Schilling erected in Rüdesheim, on the banks of the Rhine, 1883. This thirty-three-foot colossus reminded conquered France of the Prussian victory. *L'Illustration, October 6, 1883, Bibliothèque Forney, Paris.*

to their nations' exhibits, and ordinary people, lured by abundant publicity, flocked to the show.[3]

Bartholdi's world believed that noble works of the mind destined for practical use did not need to take a back seat to "purely" aesthetic creations. "The pyramids of Egypt, the hanging gardens of Babylon, the tomb of King Mausolus, the temple of Diana at Ephesus, the statue of Zeus by Phidias, the lighthouse at Alexandria, and the Colossus of Rhodes were accounted the seven wonders of the world of antiquity.... It would be a task of no small difficulty," a contemporary journalist noted, "to name seven monuments in the present era" to match those. But why, he asked, was it necessary to look only at statues and buildings to find modern marvels? "[Those] more utilitarian…might maintain that the tubular bridge over the St. Lawrence at Montreal, the Mont Cenis and St. Gothard Tunnels, Krupp's cannon foundry, the London and Northwestern Railway workshops at Crewe, Barclay & Perkins's Brewery and the London docks [are] far more astonishing illustrations of modern wealth, ingenuity, industry and power."

But the statue, said Bartholdi, no matter how huge or well engineered, must also be a work of art. It should mirror the artistic currents of its day, or at least those currents which Bartholdi chose to follow. The major schools of European painting and sculpture in the early years of the century had been loosely labeled "neoclassic" and "romantic." Neoclassic art drew its symbols and models from Greek and Roman antiquity such as the goddesses on the coinage of many nations, or the more recent statues and portraits of leaders like Napoleon and George Washington crowned with wreaths or wearing togas. The theoretical

San Carlo Borromeo. Statue by G. Crespi, erected at Arona, Italy, near Lake Maggiore, 1697. Seventy-six feet tall, the copper colossus was an inspiration to Bartholdi. With its pedestal, it towered more than one hundred and fifteen feet above the ground. Each arm measured almost thirty feet, and the statue's nose was nearly three feet long. This engraving appeared in a nineteenth-century work on colossal statues. *Ecole Nationale Supérieure des Beaux-Arts, Paris.*

Monumental lighthouses. Designs submitted for an 1852 competition held by the Ecole des Beaux-Arts in Paris. *Revue générale de l'architecture et des travaux publics, 1852. Ecole Nationale Supérieure des Beaux-Arts, Paris.*

Far right:

The tallest monuments in the world were shown in scale in this engraving, published about 1886. *Statue of Liberty National Monument, New York.*

1. Pompey's Pillar, Alexandria 105 ft.
2. Obelisk of Heliopolis, 136 „
3. Liberation Hall near Kelheim, Germany 215 „
4. The Beautiful Fountain, Nuremberg, Germany 61 „
5. The Lion of Belfort (Main Relief 46 ft.) 69 „
6. Victory Monument Freiburg, Baden 59 „
7. Emperor Wilhelm Monument 210 „
8. Nelson Column, London 161 „
9. Fountain of Victory, Paris 72 „
10. Memorial Obelisk, Munich 102 „
11. Emperor Nicholas Monument 52 „
12. Emperor Wilhelm Monument 109 „
13. Mende Fountain, Leipzig 61 „
14. Brunonia, Castle Brunswick, Germany 138 „
15. National Monument 1789
16. Emperor Alexander Mon
17. Ludwig Column Darms
18. Bavaria, Triumphal Arch
19. Empress Maria Theresa Mon
20. Carlisle Column, Eng
21. Bunker Hill Monument, C
22. Trogelthof Monument, V
23. Waterloo Column, Hanno
24. Victory Monument
25. National Monument, N
26. Grant's Tomb, New Yo
27. Arc de Triomphe, P
28. York Column, Statu

29. Constitution Column, *Stuttgart Germany* 24 ft.
30. Emperor Friedrich Monument, *Berlin* 44 „
31. Scott Monument, Edinburgh, *Scotland* 194 „
32. Grand Duke Karl Monument, *Vienna* 58 „
33. St. Mary's Column, *Leipsic, Germany* 125 „
34. Washington Column, Baltimore, Md. 182 „
35. Victory Monument, Delhi, India 246 „
36. Vendôme Column, Paris 141 „
37. Statue of the Republic, Paris 82 „
38. Battle Monument, *near New York* 230 „
39. Douglas Monument, Chicago, Ill 131 „
40. Prince Albert Monument, London 175 „
41. Farnes. Hercules, *Wilhelmshoehe* 233 „
42. Gambetta Monument, Paris 79 „

43. Emperor Trajan Column, Rome 151 ft.
44. Statue of Liberty, New York City 310 „
45. Columbus Column, Barcelona *Spain* 197 „
46. Bavaria Statue, Munich, *Germany* 95 „
47. Battle Monument, West Point N.Y. 309 „
48. Victory Monument, Berlin 202 „
49. Nelson Monument, Glasgow, *Scotland* 121 „
50. Emperor Wilhelm Nat'l Monument *Germany* 69 „
51. National War Monument, Berlin 130 „
52. War Monument, Indianapolis, Ind 262 „
53. Prince Eugen Monument, Vienna 52 „
54. Obelisk of Luxor, Paris 78 „
55. Emp. Wilhelm Monument *Germany* 213 „
56. Marcus Aurelius Column, Rome 124 „

57. Francis Fountain Prague, *Bohemia* 77 ft.
58. Fort Griswold State Monument
    Groton, Conn., U.S.A. 127 ft.
59. Garfield Memorial, Cleveland, O. 262 „
60. Congress Column, *Washington* 154 „
61. Cestius Pyramid, Rome 120 „
62. Alexander Column, St. Petersburg *Russia* 160 „
63. Arc of Peace, Milan, Italy 103 „
64. National Monument, *the Hague, Netherlands* 66 „
65. Dom Pedro Column, Lisbon *Portugal* 154 „
66. Scheldt Freedom Monument, *Antwerp, Belgium* 69 „
67. Monument to the Great Fire, London 202 „
68. July Column, Monument, Paris 154 „
69. Prince Albert Monument, *Hamburg* 82 „

70. Wellington Obelisk, Dublin 205 ft.
71. Nelson Column, Liverpool 135 „
72. Hansa Fountain, Hamburg 66 „
73. Hermann Mon't, *Teutoberg Forest, Germany* 188 „
74. Emp. Friedrich Mon't. *near Munich, Germany* 41 „
75. National Monument, Berlin 102 „
76. Column of the Grand Army, *France* 175 „
77. Obelisk of the Piazza del Popolo, Rome 112 „
78. Germania Reichstag Bldg, Berlin 151 „
79. Warriors' Mon't, *near Hildesheim, Germany* 95 „
80. Lateran Obelisk, Rome 154 „
81. Cleopatra's Needle, London 71 „
82. Victory Monument, Halle, *Germany* 64 „
83. Victory Monument, Altona 54 „

84. Emp. Wilhelm Mon't, *Coblenz Germany* 115 ft.
85. Clay's Mon't. Lexington, Ky 141 „
86. National Mon't. Mexico City 100 „
87. King Victor Emmanuel Mon't 236 „
88. Statue of St. Charles Borromeo, *near Milan, Italy* 112 „
89. Columbus Mon't, Genoa, Italy 49 „
90. Brandenburger Thor, Berlin 85 „

Monuments of Antiquity
Colossus of Rhodes 98 ft.
Statue of Nero, Rome 118 „
Sphinx of Gizeh 41 „
Memnons Statue *Memphis* 66 „

goal of neoclassic art was harmony, stillness, and perfection of form. Romantic works were more robust and dynamic, charged with emotion—like Eugène Delacroix's highly political painting of 1830, *Liberty Guiding the People*, in which a flag-waving woman in a torn dress leads a street fight at the barricades.

Both styles reflected noble ideals as well as beauty of form, and both had inspired some great works. But by the time of Bartholdi's youth neither form still attracted geniuses; merely imitators who ground out pictures, statues, and architecture in a sterile, academic style of which public officials approved.

Artists began to look for new sources of inspiration. They still drew on the myths and history of the ancient Mediterranean world. But they also looked to medieval and modern history, their native country-sides, and the exotic art of the Orient for symbols and themes through which they could express their ideas of ardent patriotism or religious mysticism. Two of these movements—Orientalism and symbolism, in which each particular element represented a particular idea—influenced Bartholdi.

Sculpture, changing more slowly than painting and in fewer new directions, was a special story. It received an added impetus from the growing power of national governments caught up in the vogue for patriotic art that marked the nineteenth century. In the words of one journalist, who titled his article "Statuemania," the "abundance of commemorative statues is a characteristic sign of this era."

European countries, particularly France, developed what amounted to an official sculpture, as political regimes paid handsomely to glorify themselves. Monuments were a fine way to do that. Empires, absolute monarchies, and dictatorships had always put up statues of their leaders to be revered. Republics, and particularly the French Republic, commemorated their own generals and politicians as well, but their monuments were supposed to be more than frozen portraits of heroes in stone or bronze. They were mainly intended to portray republican principles in some fashion or other—by the subject's background, dress, attitude, or actions. Provided one recognized the symbols, the mere presence of such a statue in a public spot could be a strong ideological statement. Bartholdi's *Lion of Belfort*, for example, announced that France had lost a war, but not its courage.

This kind of public propaganda through sculpture was an important factor in shaping the final design for the monument to liberty that Bartholdi and Laboulaye were thinking of after 1865. Additionally, there was one quality about nineteenth-century official statuary that particulary appealed to Bartholdi's expansive nature. It found its true style, its special direction, in the creation of the colossal.

Stupendous public works neatly merged classical and contemporary themes. Although they had existed in the ancient world and then disappeared, modern society now had the technology to build them again. There is evidence that all societies admire gigantic works; one only has to think of the huge, enigmatic monoliths of Easter Island or the great Buddha of Kamakura in Japan. But it was the art of ancient Mediterranean civilizations that most influenced nineteenth-century Europe. Only the monumental sculpture of Egypt had survived for modern eyes to study—but the literature of Greece and Rome was full of travelers' accounts of huge, vanished masterpieces. Often they were described in such detail that, with a little imagination, art historians had been able to make drawings of them that probably approximated their true appearance.

As befitted a classically trained artist, Bartholdi was enamored of great Graeco-Roman statuary as well as the works of ancient Egypt. He studied depictions of the acclaimed statues of Phidias of Athens, the most famous sculptor of the Periclean Age. In the workshops of the Acropolis, Phidias had produced the giant sculptures of Athena, goddess of wisdom, and of Zeus, lord of Olympus. The latter was said to be more than forty-three feet high in its seated position, crafted in wood over an iron armature and then covered with thin plates of beaten gold and carved ivory plaques.[4]

The most legendary of all these giants of antiquity was the Colossus of Rhodes. It was, according to some chronicles, a figure of the Greek god Helios 132 feet high straddling the entryway to the harbor (on the island of Rhodes) with a torch in his hand, thus serving as both an ornament and a beacon. One eighteenth-century book on historic architecture had a plate illustrating the creation. That there ever was a structure of a god bestriding a harbor so that ships could sail between his legs had no firm basis in history.[5] But the image haunted Bartholdi.

The **Lion of Belfort,** by Bartholdi, was officially inaugurated in 1880. Twenty-four meters long and sixteen meters high, the *Lion* was not, as often thought, carved from a single rock but rather constructed from numerous cut stones. *A contemporary photograph, Musée National des Techniques, Paris.*

Opposite:

Auguste **Bartholdi,** the sculptor. *Bartholdi Museum, Paris.*

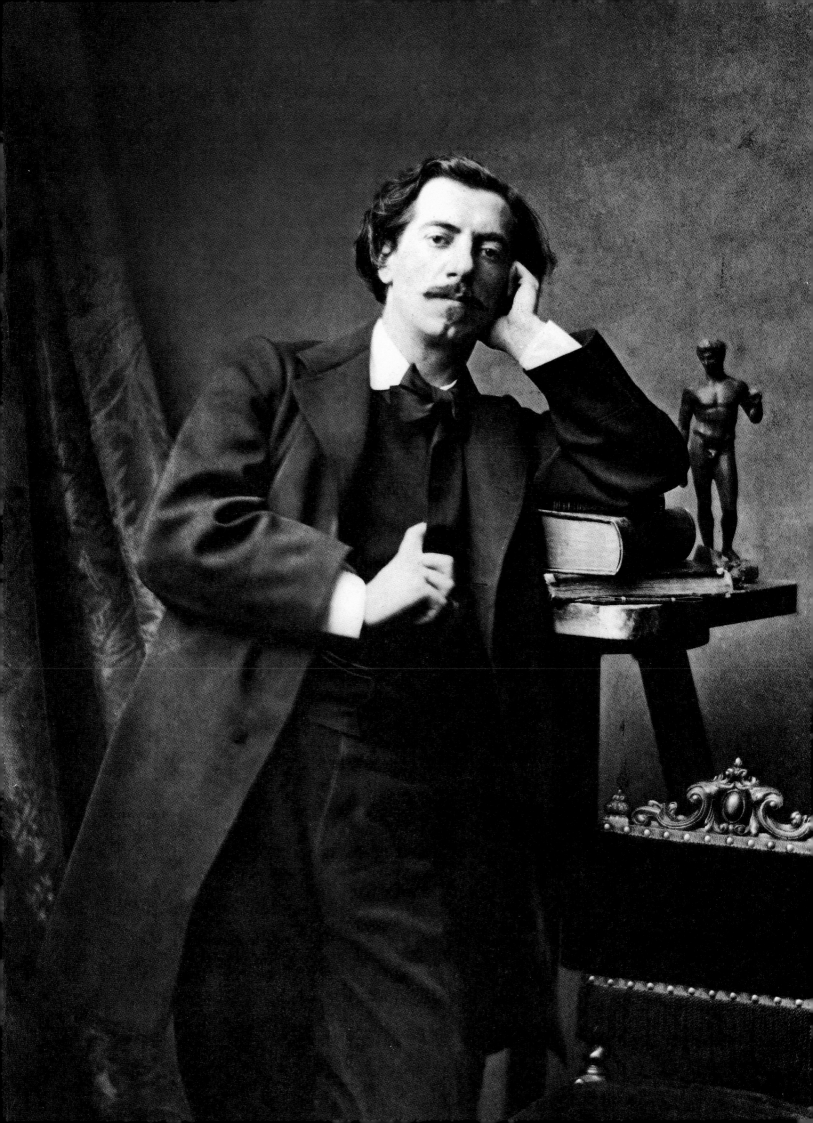

Colossal sculpture, after being forgotten for nearly a thousand years, made a comeback in Europe—especially in Renaissance Italy—during the fifteenth century, and in 1697 a truly colossal statue of a saint—*San Carlo Borromeo*, by G. B. Crespi—was erected in Arona, near Lake Maggiore. It was seventy-six feet high and stood atop a pedestal nearly forty feet tall. The work was remarkable not only for its size, but because it was created from thin plates of hammered copper, the same basic technique Bartholdi, after much research, would use on his creation.

The rising tide of nationalism in the eighteenth and nineteenth centuries led Russia, England, and Germany to fall in step. A huge equestrian statue of Peter the Great went up in St. Petersburg in 1766 and an imposing figure representing *Bavaria* in Munich in 1850. After defeating the French in 1871, the Prussian government commissioned the hefty, thirty-five-foot tall *Germania* that stood on the Rhine with sword and helmet, looking westward at its humiliated enemy. French Catholics, not to be outdone by the forces of secularism, endowed several large and splendidly located statues of the Virgin Mary.

The United States did not furnish many examples of this kind of art, except possibly Thomas Crawford's statue *Armed Freedom* placed on top of the new, enlarged dome of the Capitol in Washington in 1863. There was not yet much of an American tradition of public funding for monumental art. It took more than thirty-five years, starting in 1850, to get the Washington Monument paid for and built. The Statue of Liberty would be all the more of a novelty when it appeared.

All in all, by the time of Bartholdi's Suez disappointment in 1869, there was strong evidence that the time was right for the sculptor's idea that beautiful works of art could exist outside of museums and salons. Constantly visible to the workaday public, they could serve the practical purposes of bridges or lighthouses and still carry political or other messages. And they could be as large and imposing as technical skill could make them.

In summary, there was a perceptible demand for an art that could fuse democratic, symbolic, idealistic, functional, and colossal elements into a huge, single piece of statuary. Auguste Bartholdi was perfectly in tune with those demands. When chances to design public memorials came his way, he understood and completely fulfilled the expectations of those officials who commissioned him. The Laboulaye project was the greatest of all his commissions. It was so totally suited to him that it was only a question of time before he would throw himself into it.

But first the events of 1870 had to run their sad course. The Franco-Prussian War was a disaster for

Alexander the Great. Design for a colossal statue at Mount Athos by the architect Deinocrates about 300 B.C. *Entwurf einer historischen Architektur, J. B. Fischer von Erlach, Leipzig, 1725.* Ecole Nationale Supérieure des Beaux-Arts, Paris.

Bartholdi. It was Napoleon III's personal war, but when it ended so quickly for the Emperor with his capture in September, the provisional Republic that replaced him kept up the fighting for another futile few months. Bartholdi took a brief part in it. He enlisted in a unit commanded by the Italian patriot Giuseppe Garibaldi, a popular military leader and sworn enemy of kings who had volunteered his services to France after Napoleon's fall. But defeat was inevitable, and in the peace treaty Napoleon lost Bartholdi's homeland. The artist never forgave him and after resettling in Paris, he refused ever to go back to Colmar except for brief visits to his mother. He thought of her as living in occupied territory, and of himself as an exile. The war had politicized him. And although he had not been a particularly outspoken libertarian before 1870, he was by the spring of 1871 emotionally committed to the republican cause.

Perhaps that was why his interest in the American monument was rekindled. Or is there a more cynical explanation? Was he simply looking for new commissions and thinking that he might be able to transform his failed Egyptian project into a success? As early as 1870, he began to work on some of the small terracotta models of "Progress Bringing the Light to Asia" and transformed them into sketchy figures labeled "Liberty." For whatever reason, six years after the idea of a Franco-American memorial to independence was first discussed, Bartholdi decided to visit the United States and do some groundwork for the project. On May 8, 1871, he wrote to Laboulaye, saying he had "read and reread" the scholar's works on America, and although he began with an almost casual reference to simply "taking the air abroad," he soon got down to asking for specific help: "It occurred to me that this is a good moment to make that trip which I had the honor of discussing with you, and I am now ready to go to the United States at the end of this month! I am therefore coming to you, dear Sir, for that important support which you were good enough to promise me; I come to ask for letters of introduction that will give me standing with the press, the government and associations. I hope to make some connections with art lovers that will lead to works important to execute, but above all, I hope to succeed in realizing my plan for the monument in honor of Independence…. I will try especially to glorify the Republic and Liberty over there, hoping that I will one day find them back here, if possible. I hope, on my return, to find my poor France a little relieved of those angry, many-colored boils that formed and burst because of the Empire."

Laboulaye gave him letters of introduction, and on June 8, Bartholdi sailed aboard the steamer *Pereire*. The sculptor promised to study America and report back to Laboulaye his impressions. In conversations with Americans, Bartholdi would stress that the creation of a monument would be a common undertaking, in memory of the long-standing friendship between France and the United States.

Following pages:

Niagara Falls. Watercolor by Bartholdi, painted about 1871. *Bartholdi Museum, Colmar.*

Sequoia Forest. Watercolor by Bartholdi, painted about 1871. *Bartholdi Museum, Colmar.*

Study for a lighthouse at Suez, "Progress (or Egypt) Bringing the Light to Asia." Planned for the entrance to the canal, this study prefigured *Liberty Enlightening the World.* Watercolor by Bartholdi, 1867–1869. *Bartholdi Museum, Colmar.*

Bartholdi had a practical artist's eye for the appropriateness of the right setting, and when he first saw New York Harbor on the morning of the twenty-first, he knew in an instant, intuitive flash that it was the perfect place for the monument. The physical spectacle of the bay dazzled him: "The image presented to the sight of a passenger arriving in New York is splendid, when, after some days of voyaging, the pearly dawn of a marvelous morning reveals the magnificent scene of these great cities [New York and Brooklyn], these rivers stretching as far as the eye can see, festooned with masts and steamboats…when one awakens in the midst of that interior sea covered with vessels which swarm like a crowd in a public square."

Overwhelmed by the sensation of discovery, of coming upon an opening to new and inviting realms, he made a quick decision. "If I myself felt that spirit here," he later wrote, "then it is certainly here that my statue must rise; here where people get their first view of the New World, and where liberty casts her rays on both worlds." He even had the exact place, a little island that had caught his eye. He wrote Laboulaye: "I've found an admirable spot. It is Bedloe's Island, in the middle of the bay. I've made a little drawing of the work as it would look when emplaced there. The island belongs to the government; it's on national territory, belonging to all the States, just opposite the Narrows, which are, so to speak, the gateway to America."[6] In his ebullience, Bartholdi spoke as if the island were already his to build the statue on, little suspecting the efforts that would be required to secure it.

The drawing that he enclosed with his letter showed a robed woman holding a torch high—a slightly modified version of his figure of "Progress" for the Suez Canal.[7] This embryonic portrait of "Liberty" may have surprised Laboulaye, who had been thinking of an essentially political monument whose focus would be on Franco-American friendship, whereas the sculptor was now leaning toward something of much wider symbolic appeal, "a work of profound moral worth." But in time Bartholdi would bring Laboulaye around to approving his design.

Once ashore in New York, Bartholdi plunged into a hectic travel schedule. Though he had fallen in love at first sight with the gateway to America, his first impressions of the whole country were somewhat mixed. After a month he wrote to Laboulaye: "The vista of New York deeply impressed me. I greatly admire the institutions of the country, the patriotism, the sense of civic duty, the objectivity of the government. But meanwhile, my old European 'envelope' is a little rumpled by the materialism that prevails. American life seems to leave no time to live; their habits, their schedules, are not to my taste. Everything is big here—even the peas, that is to say, things that I prefer to be small. Everything is practical but, in a sense, collective. Society marches like trains on rails, but isolated coaches, in order to move, also have to get on the rails. The lone individual can't escape. He has to live in this 'collectivity.' There are probably elements of great power in this nation, but the individual…lives like a drop in a rainstorm, unable to break away by clinging to a blade of grass."

He crisscrossed the continent by rail, writing frequently to his mother, as well as to Laboulaye and others. It was an exciting time in which to see an America bursting with growth and energy. People were hard at work in the mines, forests, prairies, and ranches of the trans-Mississippi West, and in the factories of the growing cities. Everywhere Bartholdi saw bustle and prosperity, business adventures, startling inventions, and social excitement. He took in the whole scene—the older cities like Philadelphia, New York, Boston, and Washington, and the half-raw boomtowns of the West—Chicago, Denver, Salt Lake City, San Francisco. He was impressed, too, by the colossal wonders of nature in America, such as Niagara Falls and the Californian sequoias. However much the American pace might "rumple" his French ways, Bartholdi enjoyed the booster spirit that infused the United States.

More important, he began to learn how to use it for his own ends. Armed with Laboulaye's reputation and letters of introduction, he went looking for "persons who could take part in the work," and "help this show of friendship succeed." He found them everywhere. He met President Ulysses S. Grant; America's unofficial poet laureate, the aging Henry Wadsworth Longfellow; the distinguished and powerful senator Charles Sumner of Massachusetts; and dozens of others who were at the center of American opinion-making. There was hardly an important hand he did not shake. In every city he visited, he sought out the local "best people," and stimulated the formation of small groups of interested citizens to promote the

BIRTH OF A SYMBOL

37

Liberty in place on Bedloe's Island. Watercolor by Bartholdi, 1885. *Bartholdi Museum, Colmar.*

Study for the pedestal, watercolor sketch by Bartholdi, 1880. The truncated pyramid would be kept in principle but would be reduced in size. *Bartholdi Museum, Colmar.*

From "Progress" to "Liberty": studies by the artist in terra-cotta, 1867–1870. *Bartholdi Museum, Colmar.*

Top:

Faith. Statue by Santo Varni, about 1850. *Staglieno Cemetery, Genoa.*

Above:

Liberty. Statue by Pio Fede, 1883. *Santa Croce Church, Florence.*

Right:

Faith. Statue by Canova, 1787–1792. Detail of a monument to Pope Clement XIII at Saint Peter's Basilica, Rome. *Ecole Nationale Supérieure des Beaux-Arts, Paris.*

Far right:

Religion. Statue by Canova, 1814. *Ecole Nationale Supérieure des Beaux-Arts, Paris.*

project. Bartholdi took to public relations and promotion like a born Yankee, and after he had been at it for a few months, he could have given lessons to any American.

By the time Bartholdi got back to France early in 1872, he already had a shrewd enough sense of America's practical turn of mind to realize that some kind of gesture from the French would be needed to keep interest alive in the United States. There had to be some tangible evidence of progress; something that would, in the words of a French-language newspaper published in New York, allow "those who would eventually pay for it [the statue] to see what they were paying for."

Bartholdi wanted Laboulaye to provide some kind of spark to kindle a fire in America and announce the start of a fund-raising campaign. But the timing was wrong. In 1872 neither Laboulaye's moderate republican supporters, who had yet to win secure control of the government, nor the French people, who were being heavily taxed to pay off the enormous war indemnity to the Prussians, were in a position to respond with energy or cash. It would be 1875 before the Third Republic replaced the "provisional" government that had ruled since the fall of Napoleon III. And until then no real effort could begin.

However, the intervening three years were not to be lost time. Bartholdi was fully engaged with planning his conception. He continued to sculpt other busts and statues to earn a living but kept drawing sketches and making models of the statue so when the time for collecting contributions and beginning construction did come, everyone would know what the statue would look like. Bartholdi referred to it as "my American." But the formal title he settled on was "Liberty Enlightening the World." Gradually he convinced the circle of Laboulaye's friends who frequented Glatigny—and who would have to sell the idea to all France—that this was the appropriate theme for the monument.

The sculptor's studio. On the rear wall is a sunburst—his family's crest—and a model of the Statue of Liberty. *Bartholdi Museum, Colmar.*

But what would "Liberty Enlightening the World" look like? How did an artist give visible form to such an abstraction? Month by patient month, Bartholdi worked out his ideas.

He had no doubts about the general form of the statue. It would conform to the demands stated in 1878 by Charles Blanc, art critic and former administrative director of the Beaux-Arts school: "When a figure rears itself above the sea at the entryway to a harbor, and will be seen from a distance by navigators on one side and those who live on the seashore on the other, it is important that its mass be compact, indivisible—in a manner of speaking without a single noticeable jutting salient, without any detached accessory, without any gap. And more, so that the statue can be 'read easily' at the distance at which it will be seen, it is essential that its movement be simple and that it display in silhouette almost unbroken lines, …and in the actual model, major planes in which individual planes are dissolved and lost."

The grand outline, then, was easily decided on. But the job of choosing Liberty's individual attributes was more delicate. Bartholdi searched and hesitated a long time. There were several classical models to draw from. In Roman antiquity, for example, Liberty was represented by a woman, who might be seated, though more often she was standing. In one hand she held a Phrygian cap, the headgear that a slave received when elevated to the status of freedman. In the other, she might hold a scepter as a sign that its holder was his own master. At her feet there could be a cat, a symbol of independence; or broken shackles; or a shattered pitcher, which stood for the state of servitude that was now ended.

Of these elements, only the Phrygian cap had survived the centuries and was still shown as an essential attribute in modern representations of Liberty. This traditional emblem of the French Revolution created a problem. The cap came to be associated with the more radical and bloodthirsty developments of the

Libertas Americana. Liberty wears her hair loose in this bronze medal, designed by Benjamin Franklin in 1782. *Musée National de la Coopération franco-américaine, Blérancourt.*

Columbia. In this representation, published in *Harper's Weekly* during the 1876 Centennial celebrations, an Indian headdress has replaced the Phrygian cap. *American Library in Paris.*

Right:

Columbia. Often associated with Liberty, Columbia sometimes shares her iconography. This copper weathervane, made before 1867, shows her wearing the Phrygian bonnet. *Private Collection, New York.*

Opposite:

Coiffure a l'Indépendance or The Triumph of Liberty, one of a series of eighteenth-century prints incorporating political references into satires on the hairstyles of the day. *Musée National de la Coopération franco-américaine, Blérancourt.*

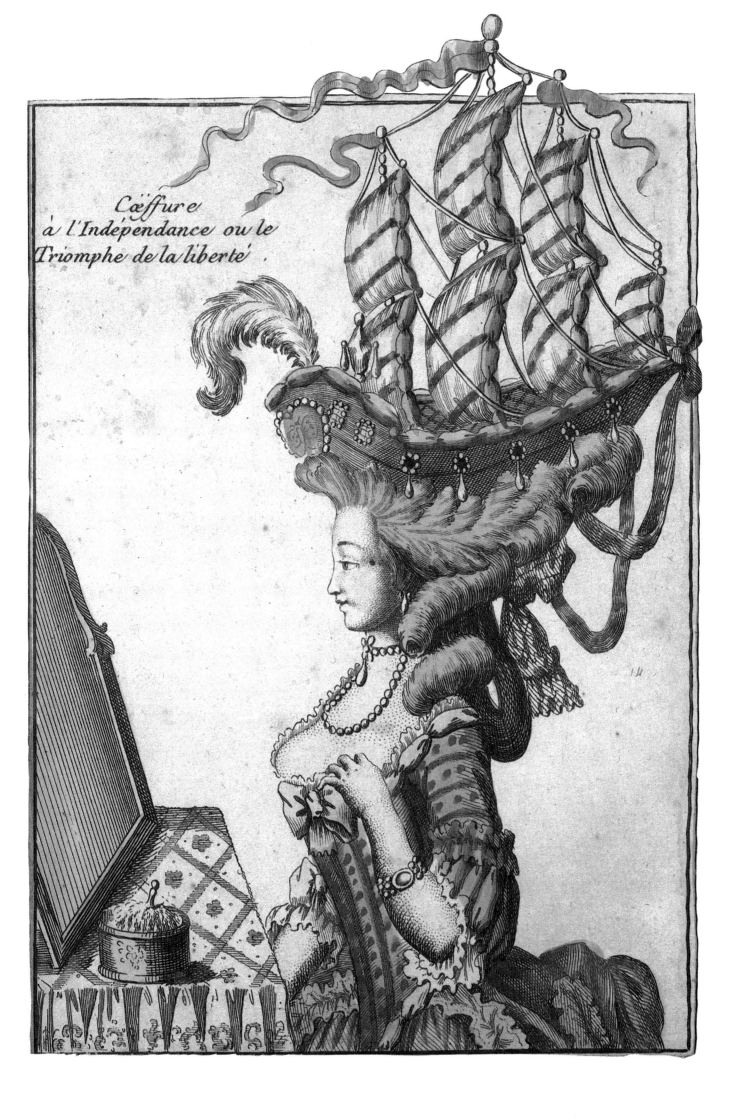

Cœffure
à l'Indépendance ou le
Triomphe de la liberté.

Liberty on top of the world and above the storms. This engraving, made for a drawing by Bartholdi, appeared in the *Irish World Centennial Supplement*, July 1876. *Private Collection, Paris.*

France crowning Art and Industry. Originally designed for the pediment above the entrance to the Palais de l'Industrie in Paris, the statue was made in 1855 by Elias Robert. Its headpiece had seven rays, and in its attitude, dress, and facial features it prefigured the future Liberty. *Parc de Saint Cloud, Paris.*

Revolution, and even republicans in France came to see it more as a sign of social anarchy rather than freedom. In the United States, when Thomas Crawford created his statue of *Armed Freedom* for the new dome of the Capitol in 1863, he gave it such a cap, but the architect of the Capitol, with congressional backing, made him replace that "bizarre headdress" with an Indian bonnet of feathers.

The memory of the violent and bloody end of the Paris Commune finally convinced Bartholdi and his backers to reject this traditional accessory as too provocative to be worn by the statue.[8]

Bartholdi later allowed a legend to circulate that his vision of the Liberty lady was partly inspired by the memory of a street riot he had witnessed in 1851 at the beginning of the Second Empire. He said he had seen a brave young woman shot down by the guns of law and order. But if that scene had really influenced him, his Liberty would have been more impetuous and closer to Delacroix's *Liberty Leading the People*. That was not what Bartholdi was after. He wanted something of the serenity of the Egyptian colossi. And Laboulaye, still eager to convince Frenchmen that a republic did not mean radical upheaval, wanted a figure that would stress prudence and legality.[9]

Another important element that went into the final version of the statue was the influence of Freemasonry on republican thought. The Freemasonry movement in France had encouraged pro-American sentiments since the end of the eighteenth century. The Lodge of the Nine Sisters, which brought the Enlightenment to philosophers of both countries, played a more-than-minimal part in the creation of the Union, and Lafayette belonged to the lodge known as The Friends of Humanity.

In the middle of the nineteenth century, the Masonic lodges of France were closely involved with liberal political movements. Sometimes taking even more radical positions than Laboulaye was willing to defend, the lodges served as rallying centers for many spirited liberals who were struggling, during the early 1870s, to consolidate the republican regime.

The historian Henri Martin, Master of a Masonic lodge, and an important future backer of the statue, was one of the regular visitors to Glatigny. Bartholdi met him there, and joined the Lodge of Alsace-Lorraine located in Paris on his return from the United States. It was no accident that this particular lodge carried the name of Bartholdi's native province and of Lorraine, also in the Prussian grip after 1871. The lodge welcomed "writers, politicians and men of ideas whose patriotism was ardent, and who wished to keep alive in their souls the cult of the 'lost provinces' and the stubborn desire for revenge."

Because of Bartholdi's membership, Masonic officials were frequently involved with the creation of the statue, and in the various ceremonies that were dedicated to it—most notably the laying of the cornerstone of the pedestal in New York in 1884. And it seems very likely that Masonic symbols were incorporated into the statue's final form by Bartholdi. For example, an issue of the magazine *The Free Mason*, founded in 1847, displays on its cover a woman lifting a flambeau and holding in her left hand the unrolled scroll of "the Law." Even more, the frontispiece of the magazine *The Chain of Union*, which the major Masonic organization of France published at that time, represents Truth as a woman perched on top of the world. She is holding a mirror, a Masonic symbol of truth, in her right hand, and a triangle, their symbol of justice, in her left. Other visible Masonic symbols are the five-pointed star on her head, and the sun behind her. And on the pedestal is written: "I Emancipate. I Pacify. I Enlighten."

"I Emancipate" describes the actual work that liberty traditionally performs in the world. "I Enlighten" is reechoed in the statue's full name of *Liberty Enlightening the World*. Bartholdi and Laboulaye believed it important to stress that the purpose of the beacon-flame in her hand was to give light, not to set fires. It was one of several iconographic elements in the statue that were pointedly conservative. Laboulaye explained it in a speech in 1876: "The statue is well named; she is truly Liberty, but American Liberty. She is not Liberty with a red cap on her head and a pike in her hand, stepping over corpses. Ours, in one hand holds the torch,—no, not the torch that sets afire, but the flambeau, the candle-flame that enlightens. In her other, she holds the tablets of the Law.... This statue, symbol of liberty, tells us at one and the same time that Liberty lives only through Truth and Justice, Light and Law. This is the Liberty

Le flambeau, non la torche.

The candle flame, not the torch. Frontispiece of a French Masonic publication. *Bibliothèque du Grand Orient de France, Paris.*

Truth holds up a mirror in the frontispiece of *La Chaine d'Union*, a publication of the Grand Lodge of France in the years from 1860 to 1870. *Bibliothèque du Grand Orient de France, Paris.*

General Lafayette. Bartholdi's statue of the famous French commander who came to America's aid during the Revolutionary War was erected in Union Square, New York City, in 1876. This engraving appeared in the *Daily Graphic* the following day. *Private Collection, Paris.*

Vercingétorix. Bartholdi's rough model, or maquette, for a monument erected at Clermont-Ferrand in 1869. *Bartholdi Museum, Colmar.*

that we desire, and that will remain forever the emblem of the alliance between America and France."

And even the "I Pacify" in the illustration on the cover of *The Chain of Union* had an echo in the early solicitations for money to build the statue. It was supposed to stand not only for liberty and enlightenment, but for peace. Again, in Laboulaye's words spoken at a subscribers' banquet: "She will not resemble those colossi in bronze, so long admired, and of which it is noted proudly that they are cast from cannon taken from the enemy.... *Our* statue will be made of pure copper, the fruit of labor and of peace."

Seen in this context, certain attributes of the composition stand out and take on added meaning. The torch is not being brandished, but rather held aloft serenely, without passion. It is the parallel of the Masonic mirror that reflects Truth. Both torch and mirror are givers of light, not destroyers. In keeping with Masonic tradition, Bartholdi could have put a mirror in the statue's other hand, but the sense remained the same even though he put the tablet of the Law there instead.

Lafayette and Washington, by Bartholdi. This sculpture was erected December 2, 1895, in the place des Etats-Unis, in Paris. *Photograph from Comet's/Jean-Claude Planchet.*

In finding a substitute for the Phrygian cap, Bartholdi elected a crown with rays. There were many possible explanations for this choice. The sunburst was a heraldic emblem of the Bartholdi family. Also, such a crown had been shown on various representations of France, Liberty, and the Republic since 1848. It had a Christian ancestry as well. One of the statues best known to Bartholdi's contemporaries was *Faith*, executed by Antonio Canova in the 1780s for the tomb of Pope Clement XIII, which featured a woman holding a cross and wearing a rayed crown. In ancient times, emperors had sometimes been shown with rayed crowns, as did the traditional depictions of the Colossus of Rhodes, which so fired Bartholdi.

Perhaps most significant, the sun was also an important Masonic symbol, and that may explain Bartholdi's choice, particularly in the light of one sentence of Masonic ritual that ran: "The Great Architect of the Universe has given the Sun to the world to enlighten it, and Liberty to sustain it." How fitting it would be to give that idea visible form by crowning Liberty with the sun's rays.

There is evidence that Bartholdi was divided between a basic attraction to the symbols of antiquity and a fascination with his newfound intellectual discoveries in the esoteric realms of Freemasonry. Until mid-1875, he thought of putting the links of a "classical" broken chain in Liberty's left hand. But the diplomacy of Laboulaye and the urgings of the Freemasons made him agree instead to change the position of the arm and put into its crook the book representing the Law, an idea both conservative and Masonic.[10] Inscribing the date of July 4, 1776, on it was a later notion, to reemphasize the special American meaning of the statue and in probable hopes of awakening American generosity in raising funds for the project.

Those classic broken chains remained on Bartholdi's mind. They were tempting because they were so eminently recognizable, as a standard image of freedom in the popular art of the time. A statue that drew considerable crowds at the Philadelphia Centennial Exposition, *The Liberation of the Blacks*, for example, showed broken chains lying at the feet of an exulting freed slave, who also held in his hand his own "table of the law" in the form of the Emancipation Proclamation. But in the end chains remained too dynamic, too narrowly literal, too "free at last!" for the broad moral statement Bartholdi wanted to make. In successive designs he put them around the statue's feet and finally moved them under the robe until they were almost completely hidden. His giantess would be as little of an incitement to future revolution as possible.

Each attribute of the statue as it finally appeared embodied the *idea* of liberty. And, as a French journalistic admirer of the work noted, "The idea here is loftier than the statue, for however astonishing the proportions of the colossus, she would remain small if it were not that she is expressing a mighty thought. Grandeur is a quality of spirit."

But it was still necessary to execute the idea. Bartholdi was incessantly preoccupied with the question of what medium to use. Neither bronze nor stone could be employed for a statue of such proportions. He needed a material that was lighter and more malleable. The biggest existing example of statuary to which Bartholdi could refer for information was the *San Carlo Borromeo* at Arona. Its sculptor, Crespi, had used the technique of copper *repoussé*—that is, he had formed his statue by hammering thin plates of copper into the shape he wanted and then joining them together. The interior of the statue was filled by a heavy masonry pier, with room left for a staircase; the projecting arm contained a metallic armature.

Jeanne-Emilie Baheux de Puysieux, Bartholdi's wife, painted by Jean Brenner. *Bartholdi Museum, Colmar.*

Opposite:

Bartholdi's mother. Portrait by Ary Scheffer. *Bartholdi Museum, Colmar.*

The *repoussé* technique was an ancient one that had been revived in modern times because it had several advantages, especially for large-scale works. It was economical, and it was malleable enough to allow the artist a facility of execution that gave him more room for originality.[11]

The great specialist in providing artists of the 1870s with the space, tools, labor, and expertise to do works in copper *repoussé* was Emile Gaget, a Parisian neighbor of Bartholdi's. He was a partner in the firm of Gaget, Gauthier and Company, whose workshops were in the city at 25 rue de Chazelles. The firm had only recently completed several works of architecture and sculpture using the technique, among them a new dome for the Opera and a twenty-two-foot-high equestrian statue of the Gallic chieftain Vercingétorix by François Millet. It did not take many conversations with Gaget to convince Bartholdi that he should use copper for the statue, and build it in the Gaget and Gauthier shops.

When all calculations were completed, it turned out that the plates of copper would need to be about an eighth of an inch thick. That left the problem of designing an interior armature to which they would be fastened. Unhesitatingly, the sculptor decided that the man he had to have for the job was his friend Eugène Viollet-le-Duc, the most in-vogue architect of the day, who was very partial to colossal works.[12] As it happened, however, Viollet-le-Duc, best remembered for his Gothic restorations, died in 1879 before he had begun the skeleton of the statue. Bartholdi then gave the assignment to Gustave Eiffel.

Finally Bartholdi was ready to look for a model for Liberty. He wanted her to have an image as noble and imposing as the great subject itself, yet with other appealing qualities—charm, serenity, the lure of the promised land, the sadness of occupied Alsace. It would have been entirely in character for him to think of using his mother's face. And in 1884, at a banquet for the sculptor, a member of the French senate told this anecdote: "Several days after having met Bartholdi for the first time the sculptor invited me to the Opera. In entering the loge, I noticed an aged woman sitting in a corner, and when the light fell on her face, I turned to Bartholdi and said to him: 'Why, that's your model for the Statue of Liberty!' 'Yes,' he answered calmly. 'It's my mother.'"

Reportedly, Bartholdi's eyes filled with tears during the recital of this tale, though he said not a word. And there is some resemblance between portraits of Madame Bartholdi and the face of the statue.

But on the other hand there are other, and competing, legends. One is that the model for the body, or as much of it as is revealed by the ample robes of the statue, was a young middle-class Alsatian woman named Jeanne-Emilie Baheux de Puysieux. That is a very romantic story, because Bartholdi married Jeanne-Emilie on December 21, 1876, at Newport, Rhode Island. Unfortunately for its truth, Mlle. Baheux was orphaned when young, and taken by her adoptive parents to Canada in 1871. From there she came to the United States, where Bartholdi met her—almost certainly for the first time—on his 1871 trip. When he came back in 1876 the friendship was renewed and ripened into love and marriage. But since he completed the model of the statue precisely during those five years of separation, it is hard to see how she could have posed for him.

Another speculation is that the face of the statue was that of Mrs. Isaac Merrit Singer, the widow of the inventor of the sewing machine, who settled in Paris in 1878 and remarried into high society. But that date, too, is far too late. The head was actually completed that summer, after many months of work. An American newspaper once quoted an anonymous "Parisian writer" to the effect that a Chicago girl had posed for Liberty's foot—presumably on one of Bartholdi's American visits.

Bartholdi never authenticated any of these stories, either from playfulness, lack of interest, or a keen awareness that such lingering doubts heightened interest in the project. The secret, if there is one, died with him. Anyway it is more likely that no "proper" woman of the 1870s would have dared pose for an artist—except for a bust of herself to stand in a drawing room. And there is a piquant though unverifiable version offered by the French author of a book entitled *La Bourgeoisie Absolue*: Bartholdi did what any sculptor would have done in that case, he hired a model. Her name was Céline, and she frequented Pigalle.

So is it some lovely unknown woman of the people who incarnates Liberty? Is it the artist's mother? Or is it a girl of the streets?

UNION FRANCO-AMÉRICAINE

SOUSCRIPTION
POUR L'ÉRECTION D'UN MONUMENT COMMÉMORATIF
DU
CENTIÈME ANNIVERSAIRE
DE L'INDÉPENDANCE DES ÉTATS-UNIS
ÉRIGÉ EN SOUVENIR DE L'ANCIENNE AMITIÉ DE L'AMÉRIQUE ET DE LA FRANCE
PAR LES AMIS DES DEUX NATIONS

L'Amérique va célébrer prochainement le centième Anniversaire de son indépendance. Cette date marque une époque dans l'histoire de l'humanité : au Nouveau Monde, elle rappelle son œuvre, la fondation de la grande République; à la France, une des pages qui font le plus d'honneur à son histoire.

De concert avec nos amis des États-Unis, nous pensons que c'est une occasion solennelle d'associer la France et l'Amérique dans une commune manifestation. Malgré la distance des temps, les États-Unis aiment à se rappeler une ancienne fraternité d'armes; toujours on honore chez eux le nom de la France. Le grand événement que l'on doit fêter le 4 juillet 1876 nous permet de célébrer avec nos frères d'Amérique la vieille et forte amitié qui unit longtemps les deux peuples.

Le Nouveau Monde s'apprête à donner à cette fête une splendeur extraordinaire; des amis des États-Unis ont pensé que le génie de la France devait s'y montrer sous une forme éclatante. Un artiste français a traduit cette pensée dans un projet digne de son but et qui a réuni tous les suffrages; il s'est mis d'accord avec nos amis d'Amérique et a préparé tous les moyens d'exécution.

Il s'agit d'élever, en souvenir du glorieux Anniversaire, un monument exceptionnel. Au milieu de la rade de New-York, sur un îlot qui appartient à l'Union des Eats, en face de Long-Island, où fut versé le premier sang pour l'Indépendance, se dresserait une statue colossale, se dessinant sur l'espace, encadrée à l'horizon par les grandes cités américaines de New-York, Jersey-City et Brooklyn. Au seuil de ce vaste continent, plein d'une vie nouvelle, où arrivent tous les navires de l'Univers, elle surgira du sein des flots; elle représentera : « LA LIBERTÉ ÉCLAIRANT LE MONDE. » La nuit, une auréole lumineuse, partant de son front, rayonnera au loin sur la mer immense.

Ce monument sera exécuté en commun par les deux peuples, associés dans cette œuvre fraternelle, comme ils le furent jadis pour fonder l'Indépendance. Nous ferons hommage de la statue à nos amis d'Amérique : ils se joindront à nous pour subvenir aux frais de l'exécution et de l'érection du monument qui servira de piédestal.

Nous affirmerons ainsi, par un souvenir impérissable, l'amitié que le sang versé par nos pères avait scellée jadis entre les deux nations.

Réunissons-nous pour célébrer cette fête des peuples modernes : il nous faut être nombreux pour donner à cette manifestation l'élan qu'elle doit avoir, afin d'être digne du passé. Que chacun apporte son obole; les plus faibles souscriptions seront bien accueillies. Que le nombre des signataires témoigne des sentiments de la France.

Les listes seront réunies en volumes pour être offertes à nos amis d'Amérique.

Reconnaissants de l'amitié dont on veut bien les honorer aux États-Unis, les membres du Comité directeur ont accepté la mission de prendre l'initiative du mouvement : il sera grandement suivi de l'autre côté de l'Océan. Nous espérons recueillir partout de sympathiques adhésions.

SUBSCRIPTION
FOR THE BUILDING OF A COMMEMORATIVE MONUMENT
OF THE
CENTENNIAL ANNIVERSARY
OF UNITED STATES INDEPENDANCE
ERECTED IN REMEMBRANCE OF THE ANCIENT FRIENDSHIP OF FRANCE AND AMERICA
BY THE FRIENDS OF BOTH NATIONS

America will very soon celebrate the centennial anniversary of her Independance. This date marks an epoch in human history : to the New World, it records its sublime work the foundation of the grand Republic; to France one of the most honourable pages of her history.

We believe, as well as our friends of the United States, that it affords a solemn occasion to unite France and America in a common manifestation. Notwithstanding the long past time, the United States like to recall to mind an ancient fraternity in arms; the name of France is always honoured by them. The great event which will be performed the 4 july 1876, permits us to celebrate with our American friends the old and sincere friendship which so long united both nations.

The New World is preparing to give to this great festival an extraordinary splendour; some friends of the United states thought that the geny of France should show itself in a cordial and striking manner. A French artist rendered that idea in a project worthy of its purpose and which has reunited all approbations; in going to America he came to an understanding with our friends and prepared all the means of execution.

The question is to elevate in commemoration of the glorious anniversary an exceptional monument. In the middle of the New-York harbour, on a little Island belonging to the Union, facing Long Island where the first blood has been shed for the Independance, will be raised a colossal statue, showing its grand figure in the space, horizoned by the large cities of New-York, Jersey City and Brooklyn. At the entrance of that vast continent, full of new life, where ships meet from all points of the world, it will look as springing up from the bosom of the deep representing : Liberty enlightning the World. At night a luminons aureola projected from the head will radiate on the far flowing waves of the Ocean.

The monument will be erected by both nations associated in this fraternal achievement as they were formerly to carry out the Independance. We shall amicably offer our American friends the statue, and they on their side will meet the expences of the piedestal.

Thus shall we consolidate by an eternal remembrance, the friendship which has been sealed by the blood of both people's forfathers.

Let us unite to celebrate this fête of modern people, we must be numerous give to this manifestation the fervour which it requires, in order to equal the ever memorable and past events. Let each one bring his obole; however trifling each person's offering may be, it will be received with thanks. Let the number of suscribers show the sentiments of France.

We shall organize our lists in volumes which will be offered to our American friends.

The members of the committee, most gratefull for the friendship with which they have been honoured in America, assumed the direction of the mouvement; the exemple will be nobly followed on the other side of the Ocean. We hope to meet with sympathetic adhesions everywhere.

CHAPTER TWO

FROM SHORE TO SHORE

W hile Bartholdi was hard at work finding the exact combination of idea, model, and technique that would realize his dream, Laboulaye was preparing to set up the administrative and financial structure of the project. By the spring of 1875 it was clear that France was going to become permanently republican, and he could concentrate his attention on the statue. To give the project a broad base of popular support, Laboulaye wanted the statue to be paid for by the widest possible number of contributions.

His first step was to form an organization, the Franco-American Union, in April, with himself as its president. The first members were the faithful of Glatigny. As is usual in such philanthropic enterprises, a small number of them, organized as an Executive Committee and usually referred to simply as "The Committee," did most of the serious work. As is also customary, many prestigious honorary members were immediately added for public relations purposes. Chief among them were Elihu Washburne, the American ambassador to France, and Philippe Bartholdi, who in turn was France's ambassador to Washington and, by happy chance, a distant cousin of the sculptor. In addition, Ambassador Bartholdi had just been named one of France's Commissioners to the forthcoming Philadelphia Centennial Exposition. Together the two envoys were responsible for displaying products at the exposition. Another honorary American member was John W. Forney, a Philadelphia politician and journalist, who carried the resounding title of Commissioner-General of the United States in Europe for the Exposition. Additional French members included descendants of noble families as well as those of Lafayette, Tocqueville, and Rochambeau, and well-placed members of the administration and the French parliament.

The Union opened a bank account and established an office at a fashionable Paris address, and on September 28, 1875, printed its first public appeal in two Parisian newspapers. It said that the imminent centennial anniversary of American independence would mark an "epoch in human history," and that French genius should contribute to the festivities marking the occasion. "A French artist," it went on, had devised "an exceptional monument," a colossal statue for New York Harbor: "On the threshold of that vast continent, full of new life, where ships arrive from everywhere, it will rise from the waves, representing 'Liberty Enlightening the World.' " The enlightenment would be literal as well as metaphorical: "At night a luminous aureola projected from the forehead will shine far out over the vast ocean.... The monument will be erected by both nations, associated in this fraternal achievement as they were formerly to carry out the [American] independence. We shall amicably offer our American friends the statue, and they on their side will meet the expenses of the pedestal." Even the smallest contributions, readers were assured, would be gratefully received.

Within a few days this appeal had appeared in other newspapers throughout France, and the first surge of response seemed promising. Newspaper editorials were mostly favorable. Some subscriptions began to flow in, including 500 francs from the city of Rouen and 1,000 from Le Havre. A major metals manufacturer offered to provide all the necessary copper. When Bartholdi went to thank him personally, he said, with a modest smile, "I am not a prince, but I love liberty, I love America, and since I'm in a position to do it, I'd like to show that a Frenchman can match the Americans in patriotism."

Opposite:

A fund-raising appeal sent out by the French-American Committee in 1875. *Bibliothèque du Conservatoire National des Arts et Métiers, Paris.*

The Banquet at the Hôtel du Louvre, where the French-American Committee celebrated its founding on November 6, 1875. *Le Journal Illustré, November 21, 1875. Bibliothèque du Conservatoire National des Arts et Métiers, Paris.*

President Grant. *Le Journal Illustré, November 1877. Bibliothèque du Conservatoire National des Arts et Métiers, Paris.*

LETTER TO PRESIDENT GRANT

Sir:

On the solemn occasion of the anniversary of the centennial of American Independence, it occurred to us that France would like to participate in the joy of her American friends and show how she has remained faithful to her old traditions.

We have been thinking for a long time of offering to our American friends at the time of this celebration some evidence of our sentiments worthy of the genius of France.

Our idea was formulated in a splendid manner by our friend the celebrated sculptor Auguste Bartholdi, member of our committee. He went to America to study the question, he consulted with a great number of our friends, and he reached an understanding with them.

Our project would be to construct in the middle of New York Harbor on a small island belonging to the Union, across from Long Island, there where the first blood for liberty was spilt, a giant statue to Independence. The colossus would show its great silhouette against the sky, surrounded by the great cities of New York, New Jersey, and Brooklyn.

At the entrance to this vast continent filled with new life, where ships arrive from all over the world, she will seem to rise from the depths, representing Liberty Enlightening the World. At night, a luminous halo will shine from her head on the far-off waves of the ocean.

The project was submitted to your excellency three years ago by Mr. Bartholdi, who was introduced to

Flushed with high expectations, the Union scheduled a kick-off banquet at the Hôtel du Louvre on November 6, and a grand party at the Palace of Industry two weeks later. But however exhilarating these early moments might be, the Union had been wildly inaccurate in issuing its initial appeal. They had said that Bartholdi, on his American trip, had "prepared all the means of execution." In fact there was no American organization in place whatever. The French would provide the statue but it was up to the Americans to construct the pedestal and find a place to put it, if they accepted the statue in the first place. Not a sketch had been drawn and not a penny had been raised. The Union did not have the slightest assurance that the statue could be put anywhere in New York Harbor. All President Grant had told Bartholdi was that congressional approval would be necessary to get Bedloe's Island. In any event, the statue could not possibly be ready by 1876. And the lighthouse-in-the-head was a wild idea that would never be carried out.

It was not, in fact, until October 26, 1875, that Laboulaye presented a formal request for the Bedloe's Island site to President Grant through the agency of Ambassador Washburne. Washburne was a cautious politician, who did not like to stick his neck out any farther than he had to. Although he told Laboulaye he supported the project "with all his influence," the only thing Washburne did do was forward the request to the State Department, with no comments of his own. In fact, Washburne was waiting to see what the statue looked like and what its true chances of realization were before he committed himself. He had his chance at the November 6 banquet, which was supposed to bring together all of Paris.

It did not quite do that, but it was an impressive occasion all the same. The Minister of Finance and the Minister of Education were there, representing the French President, Marshal MacMahon; there were highly placed officials in the administration of Paris, and a goodly number of members of parliament. Commissioner Forney was there, and a number of men from distinguished American mercantile interests with offices in Paris. De Lesseps, the hero of the Suez Canal, who was already thinking about digging a canal through Panama, was present, enjoying a visit with Viollet-le-Duc. Also on hand were several pro-American French aristocrats who were members of the Union.

At eight-thirty the guests were admitted to the banquet room, where the party-givers demonstrated a fine sense of the theatrical. The tables were arranged in a horseshoe, with shields in the center displaying portraits of Washington, Franklin, Lafayette, Rochambeau, Lincoln, and Grant. The walls and windows were festooned with flowers, greenery, medals, and French and American flags. A model of *Liberty Enlightening the World* stood at the end of the hall, displayed against a large curtain. The first public showing was a success. The nobility of Bartholdi's conception impressed everyone and set the mood for the flow of after-dinner oratory that ended with a final toast, by Laboulaye, to the eternal friendship between France and the United States.

While the occasion was enough to bring Washburne to write a slightly more affirmative letter four days later to Secretary of State Hamilton Fish, he still hedged his bet. "The project of erecting a monument," he said, "seems to be taking considerable proportions. Although I have not myself felt certain of its success." He went on to say, nonetheless, that favorable action on the request for Bedloe's Island would be good from all points of view in France: "First, in cementing still more strongly the friendship between the two nations; second, in helping the Commission [i.e., of the Franco-American Union] to get subscriptions to complete the monument; and thirdly, it would have a beneficial influence so far as the Centennial Exhibition is concerned, by awakening a livelier interest in the whole subject."

Washburne's lack of conviction about the success of the project was not unjustified. In spite of the opening fanfare, things did not go well. A few thousand francs had been collected in the first weeks, but the gigantic project required hundreds of thousands—six hundred thousand, in fact—and after that first gush of contributions in October, the stream of money dwindled to a trickle. The gathering at the Palace of Industry failed to provoke a wave of donations. Even a subscription from Marshal MacMahon, which was trumpeted in the press, failed to speed up the pace of collection. Laboulaye turned to the community of French businessmen in New York, most of whom were members of the Cercle Français de l'Harmonie de New York (the Harmony Club). Laboulaye asked its president, Adolf Salmon, to form a kind of American subcommittee of the Franco-American Union to undertake fund raising for the statue,[1] but

you by our common friend Colonel J. H. Forney.

Mr. Bartholdi had the honor of informing your excellency of our desire to erect this monument on Bedloe's Island, site of a small fort belonging to the Union. Your excellency kindly reminded him that this matter would have to be put before Congress.

Therefore, sir, we have the honor of addressing our request to you.

Bedloe's Island is a marvelous location for the project we envision. Our monument, erected in the middle of the central courtyard, would occupy a square approximately forty feet on a side, which should not overwhelm the fort.

We offer the statue to our American friends; for their part, they will take charge of organizing a subscription to build the pedestal. Our two nations will be associated in this pious homage paid to the glory of the past just as they were united in achieving independence.

In France, we want to show our warm enthusiasm for this noble liberty which represents the glory of United States and which guides the peoples of today by its example.

We will be happy for this exchange of goodwill with the American nation, and especially insofar as our gesture will strengthen us in the work of regeneration that we seek in our own country.

We hope, sir, that your excellency will press our case favorably in Congress.

From the Franco-American Union, October 26, 1875.

The plaster model perfected by Bartholdi and approved by the French-American Committee in 1875. *Collection of the Société Miège et Buhler, Paris.*

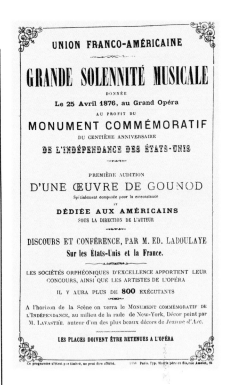

Salmon was not interested. The best that he could do was to print appeals in the leading Franco-American newspaper, the *Courier des Etats-Unis*. The response was disappointing.

At a series of anguished meetings of the Executive Committee it began to look as if the copper colossus was going to be stillborn. But then Bartholdi came up with a brilliantly imaginative plan to get the French business community involved in the project. He had two newspaper releases prepared in November 1875. The first urged manufacturers and merchants to subscribe for altruistic principles.[2] But the second showed the French merchant that he could make some money out of the project: "The Committee of the Franco-American Union has decided that the right to reproduce the Centennial monument, which is a copyrighted artistic property, will be granted to all those manufacturers, sales agents and mercantile houses which have business in the United States or any other country, and wish to associate their product with the image of this work, which is certain to become the national emblem of American independence. The price paid for this right will be turned over to the subscription fund."

It was a stroke of promotional genius, if not entirely straightforward. Bartholdi had no guarantee that his statue would in fact become "the national emblem of American independence," but within a month, scores of businessmen were signing up and paying to use the picture of the yet-unbuilt statue in their advertising.[3] By 1876 its image was splashed across billboards singing the praises of many of France's best-known products. The "great lady" turned out to be an extraordinarily successful commercial logo.

By 1876 the Committee realized it would have to send at least some part of the statue as a token gift for America's hundredth birthday, if for no other reason than to get Americans to start raising funds for the pedestal. The Committee agreed to send the hand bearing the torch in time for the opening of the Philadelphia Exposition in May.

Bartholdi began work, using what little money had already been received. Like many projects dependent on public subscriptions, the statue could only be realized piecemeal as funds were available.

To begin with, Bartholdi made a plaster model one-sixteenth the size of the full statue. When he was satisfied with the details of that, he did another twice as large, and then once again, after adjusting proportions and details to his satisfaction, did a one-quarter-sized model. This model was broken down into sections, and each section enlarged to the final dimensions.

It worked in this way: The quarter-sized section was put in a three-dimensional framework, like a box without sides, and hung with a series of plumb lines. Then precise measurements were taken from several points on the section of statue to the plumb lines. Now an identical framework four times as large as the

first was built and the measurements, when transferred to it, became a basis for a plaster enlargement over a light lath skeleton.

Bartholdi smoothed and refined this full-sized plaster portion of the statue to his satisfaction, and then workmen took heavy pieces of wood and carefully cut and shaped them until they fit snugly around the curves of the plaster. When removed, the pieces became honeycomblike wooden molds or templates of the section they had covered. What remained then was to take thin sheets of copper an eighth of an inch thick and hammer and smooth them into the templates until they formed the exact shape of the plaster original. The final statue would consist of three hundred such pieces of shaped copper riveted together.

It was painstaking work, requiring thousands of carefully verified measurements, a large crew of workers, considerable space in the Gaget and Gauthier workshops, and constant supervision by Bartholdi. Patiently, the sculptor began creating the hand and the torch in the spring of 1876. Friends, skeptics, curiosity seekers, and reporters visited the workshops to admire the gargantuan, otherworldly proportions of the hand. The index finger alone was eight feet long.

Since only a small part of the wrist would be on display, Bartholdi did not have to worry about building strong internal supports for it. But even so, the work was not finished by May, when he had to leave for America. He had been named an Adjunct Commissioner to the Exposition, a useful appointment but one that meant he had to be in Philadelphia with the rest of the French delegation as soon as possible. Reluctantly, Bertholdi had to leave his deputies in charge of the work. Shortly before his May 6 departure, however, he helped in another fund-raising gala. This was a "Musical Solemnity" that the Committee put on at the Opera to attract fresh subscriptions. Charles Gounod, the celebrated composer of *Faust*, directed a group of equally popular singers in a cantata which he had written for the occasion, naturally entitled *Liberty Enlightening the World*. Behind the chorus was a huge canvas backdrop on which an artist had painted the statue as it would look when finished and standing on its pedestal in New York.

Unfortunately, the evening was both a bore and a financial failure. But it was not a total loss.[4] When Bartholdi set sail, he took the canvas backdrop with him. It would help him to sell the statue to the Americans while the great hand and torch were being completed in Paris.

And some hard selling would be needed. Eight months after the Franco-American Union's first public announcement, there was still little concrete evidence of American interest. The Secretary of State had written to Washburne saying he doubted France's "ability to present the proposed monument." Other American government officials were worried about the eventual cost of the project. They figured that the

After the model he made to submit to the French-American Committee for their approval, Bartholdi made one about twice as large: one-sixteenth the full size and seven feet from the heel to the top of the head. This in turn would be made four times larger to arrive at a model about twenty-eight feet high. This plaster study, still reasonable enough in scale for the eye to take in, was checked and refined to correct any imperfections that had been exaggerated as the statue was enlarged. When Bartholdi was satisfied, this model was divided into parts, each of which was enlarged again by a factor of four.

To enlarge the hand, for example, Bartholdi made a square base four times larger than the base of the hand on his quarter-size model. He hung plumb lines from the rafters, and then, using rulers, compasses, and plumb lines, painstakingly transferred the shape of the model to the larger base. When he had plotted the major points of the outline, he connected them with timber and lath to make a skeleton which would eventually be covered with plaster. Each nail on the final skeleton required six measurements, three on the quarter model and three on the enlargement, not counting measurements taken for verification. Each section worked on in this way averaged ten-and-a-half feet in height, with three hundred major points to be transferred and twelve hundred secondary ones, requiring some nine thousand separate measurements per section. The hand, torch, and forearm required thirty-eight of these sections.

Right:

Enlarging Liberty. A worker takes the measurement on the quarter-model of the hand and will transfer it to the full-size plaster hand. Plumb lines hang from the top of the quarter-model and from the ceiling. *Illustrated Christian Weekly, July 8, 1876. American Library in Paris.*

Inside Gaget and Gauthier's studio, workmen put the finishing touches on the hand and torch. The intermediate-stage plaster models are visible at left. *Collection of the Société Miège et Buhler, Paris.*

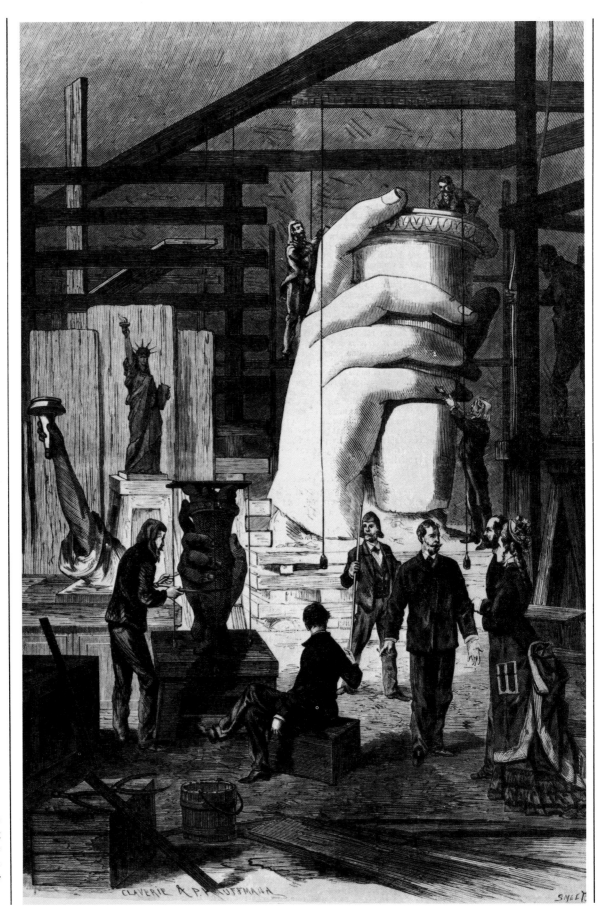

The hand arrives in Philadelphia, September 1, 1876. *L'Illustration, October 21, 1876. Bibliothèque Forney, Paris.*

Opposite:

At the Philadelphia Exposition. In spite of its late arrival, the hand and torch made a splendid impression. Photograph by E. L. Wilson and W. I. Adams, 1876. *Bibliothèque du Conservatoire National des Arts et Métiers, Paris.*

In Madison Square. After Philadelphia, the hand was sent to New York, where it would remain for four years. *Bartholdi Museum, Colmar.*

pedestal would cost at least $100,000 (it actually cost about $250,000), a large sum to raise by popular subscription when the country was still suffering from a major depression that had begun in 1873. Moreover, the Union's appeal asked only that Americans pay the expenses of the pedestal. But who would finance the work of putting the colossus on its pedestal, getting it to function as a lighthouse, and having an inaugural celebration? Few American politicians in 1876 were eager to make expensive commitments for receiving a 151-foot statue that, except for its left hand, was still on a Parisian drawing board.

If newspaper editorials were any guide, the Committee had cause for concern with the cool reception afforded to the statue by many Americans. Some of them called the proposed monument a French oddity, "almost too fantastic and too poetic ever to be realized." Some were skeptical of the theme of Franco-American unity, and took note that "Americans are, in general, more drawn towards England and even Germany than towards France." Some papers were flattered that France, so renowned for its culture, should be giving a work of art to America.[5] But transatlantic enthusiasm stopped there. For some American editors, the idea was a shade too abstract. Why, asked the New York *Herald* in 1875, shouldn't France offer a statue of Lafayette, a figure well known in the history of Franco-American relations?

What the *Herald* did not know at that time, however, was a quiet but important footnote to the story of the Statue of Liberty. The French community in New York had actually decided to present a statue of Lafayette to the city in gratitude for help extended by New Yorkers to famine sufferers during the 1870–71 siege of Paris. They had commissioned Bartholdi to do it, and it would be completed in 1876.

The New York Times took a much harder line. Should Americans pay for a pedestal for an only partly finished statue? Certainly not. "No true patriot," said the *Times* on September 29, "can support such expenditures for a bronze female in the present state of our finances."

It seemed that the springtime of 1876 was not the opportune moment for Bartholdi to win much goodwill for his colossus. Yet Bartholdi was convinced that he could win over both the American people and their government. He was betting his career on it.

Things started badly for him, however. The hand was supposed to arrive by the Fourth of July but was delayed. He knew how thoroughly all activities on America's hundredth Independence Day would be covered, and wanted desperately to have something to show. With his great skill at improvisation, he produced the canvas backdrop of the "Musical Solemnity" at the Opera. He arranged to show it at a meeting of the New York City Club in Madison Square on July Fourth. So instead of a look at part of the real statue in Philadelphia, America got only a picture of how Liberty would someday appear in New York. And yet the substitution was a success, because New York reporters gave the painting good coverage and the New York papers were more widely copied throughout the country than those of Philadelphia.

Bartholdi got more coverage when the "arm," as he referred to it in his letters, finally reached an American port on August 14, aboard the steamer *Labrador*. Reporters noted with astonishment that it took twenty men to bring its nine-by-fourteen-foot packing case ashore. The public got a clearer vision of just how huge the statue would eventually be when the hand was set up on the Exposition grounds close to the popular Hall of Machinery. It quickly became an equally powerful attraction to visitors. For a small donation that went to the Franco-American Union, they could buy a ticket to enter the arm and climb into the torch. Thousands of ordinary Americans thereby became subscribers to the great project.

The next step in Bartholdi's campaign for American support came on September 6, 1876, when his statue of Lafayette was first displayed in New York. Since it was a gift to the city, its unveiling was a public occasion. Abundant press coverage included interviews with Bartholdi, whose accessibility, ready answers to all questions, and effusive praise of the United States were making him something of a pet with American readers. While the spotlight was on him, he organized a trip to Bedloe's Island with a group of New York officials, and as the steamer *Washington* carried them across the bay, he gave a seductive talk on how perfectly Liberty would harmonize with the busy location, the vast horizons, the light-filled perspectives.

As a trump card, he managed to exploit a long-simmering civic rivalry between New York and Philadelphia. When *The New York Times* printed its diatribe against spending money for a "bronze female,"

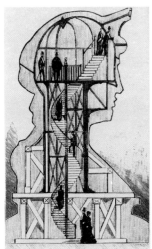

Inside Liberty's head was a winding staircase leading to windows in the crown. *L'Univers Illustré, January 5, 1878. Bibliothèque du Conservatoire National des Arts et Métiers, Paris.*

On the Champ de Mars in Paris. Liberty's head dominated the landscape at the Universal Exposition of 1878. *Collection of the Société Miège et Buhler, Paris.*

Left:

Hammering the copper. Workers shape the copper by first bending it with levers and then hammering it inside wooden molds; others finish the modeling with smaller hammers and smoothing tools. *Le Journal Illustré, May 28, 1876. Private Collection, Paris.*

Bottom left:

Modeling the head. A system of pulleys lifted buckets of plaster to the men working on the full-sized model, which measured over twenty feet high. *L'Illustration, January 5, 1878. Bibliothèque Forney, Paris.*

In front of the Pavilion of Nations. Collage by Bartholdi showing how the head would be exhibited at the 1878 Universal Exposition in Paris. *Bibliothèque du Conservatoire National des Arts et Métiers, Paris.*

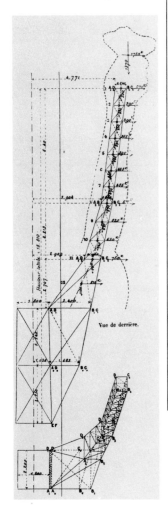

Bartholdi wrote a furious letter to the editor saying that if New York was going to be so stingy, he would place his creation in Philadelphia where a subscription committee had already been started.

There was some question whether subscription plans in Philadelphia had gotten much past the talking stage, but New Yorkers rose to the bait. First came the members of the Harmony Club, who had taken the lead in raising money for the Lafayette statue. A few days after Bartholdi's letter appeared, they met in the club's parlors, and turned their Committee for the Statue of Lafayette, which had fulfilled its purpose, into the Franco-American Union–Statue of Liberty–New York Committee, just as Laboulaye had asked for a year earlier. The intercity competition was beginning to stir things up.[6]

In spite of all the good publicity, and the creation of several local subscription committees formed in various communities, there was not yet a single, powerful nationwide organization that was working for the monument in America in the same way the Franco-American Union was doing in France. In December 1876, several powerful New Yorkers of national prominence joined the ranks. They created what was, in effect, a United States coordinating body, which was called simply The American Committee for the Statue of Liberty. Its head was William M. Evarts, who had been named as Secretary of State in the administration of Rutherford B. Hayes. Richard Butler, a New York businessman, was secretary of the American Committee and did much of the hard work. But Evarts's name added luster, as did those of Edwin D. Morgan, a former New York governor and senator; Parke Godwin, editor of the New York *Post*, then a distinguished and influential journal; and the venerated American poet William Cullen Bryant, who had been Godwin's predecessor at the *Post*. Together they gave the statue new credibility.

The American Committee began with a public appeal in the newspapers for money for the pedestal. The text was elegantly phrased. It warmly praised the French for conceiving of such a unique gift, and then came directly to the point. In response to such generosity, the American people needed "only to provide for the reception, location, presentation and inauguration of this statue." All subscriptions, "from 10 cents to $100 and more," would be gratefully received. "Chambers of commerce, boards of trade, exchanges, tradesmen's and mechanics' associations, clubs and other regular organizations" were "particularly required to interest themselves in the furtherance of [this] object."

The Committee immediately petitioned the lame duck President Grant to transmit their formal request for the donation of Bedloe's Island as the site for the statue to Congress for approval.

Grant did so, and the legislative machinery ground into gear. The mechanism was for the Senate and House duly to consider a joint resolution with the usual committee hearings, reports, and debates to "accept the offer of the French people and invite the President to designate a suitable spot on the Federal Government's properties of Bedloe's Island or Governor's Island in New York harbor" for the statue. The federal government's authority to do so rested, in part, on the assumption that the statue was going to double as a beacon. Beacons, constitutionally speaking, came under the national power to regulate commerce. So the resolution added that the President should initiate the appropriate steps for "the inauguration of the Statue and its maintenance as a lighthouse." Its floor manager in the House was another important recruit, Democrat Abram S. Hewitt, a wealthy retired iron manufacturer who would one day be mayor of New York and doubtless liked the idea of any major construction made of metal.

The resolution was passed on Washington's Birthday, 1877, and signed by President Grant on March 3, his last full day in office.

Bartholdi had not spent all his time in 1876 working. He had socialized with his growing circle of American friends, who introduced him to Jeanne-Emilie Baheux de Puysieux, an orphaned French woman living in America who was a distant cousin of the American artist John La Farge. Somehow he had found time after they were introduced to woo and win her. In a somewhat hasty marriage that just barely managed to prevent a public scandal, the two were wed in December 1876. At age forty-two, Bartholdi still felt the need, however, to write a lengthy and apologetic letter to his mother informing her of the match. He explained that although Jeanne lacked the wealth and social connections necessary to further his career—as Madame Bartholdi obviously expected in her son's wife—she would make up for it by her selfless devotion to his every need and lifelong success. It was a prediction that proved to be true.

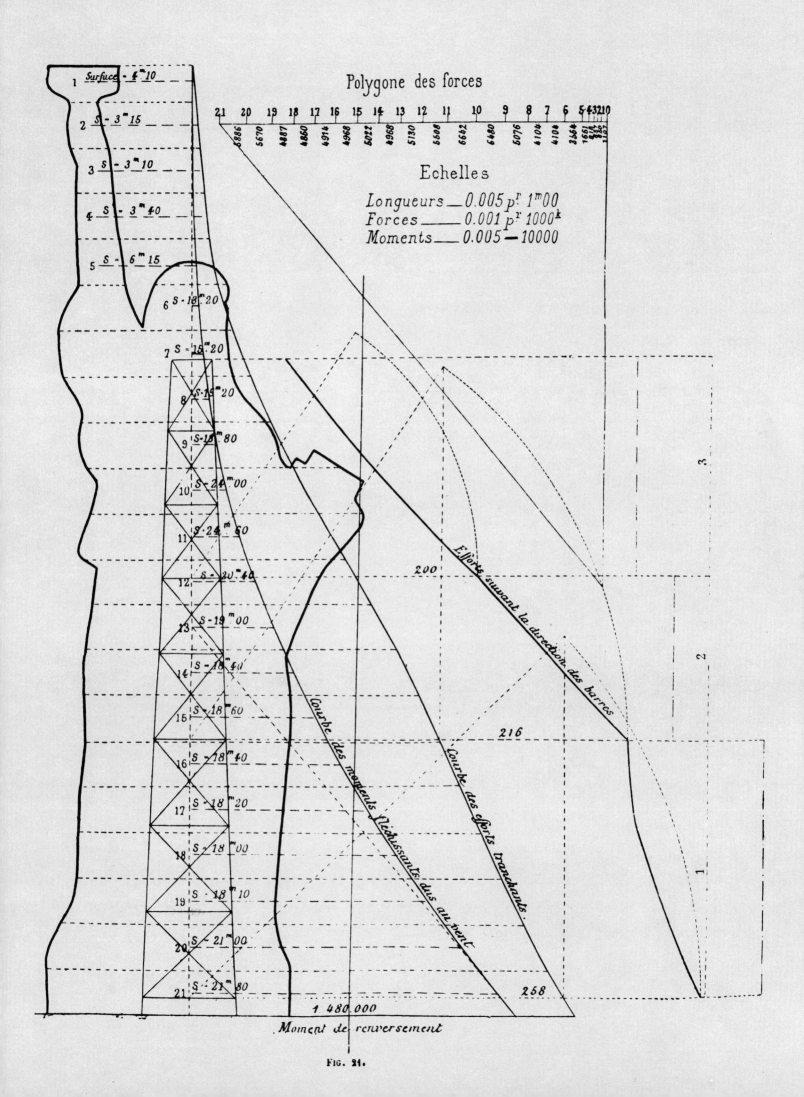

Polygone des forces

Echelles
Longueurs ___ 0.005 p.r 1m00
Forces _____ 0.001 p.r 1000k
Moments ___ 0.005 — 10000

Surface - 4m 10
S - 3m 15
S - 3m 10
S - 3m 40
S - 6m 15
S - 18m 20
S - 15m 20
S - 15m 20
S - 15m 80
S - 24m 00
S - 24m 60
S - 20m 40
S - 19m 00
S - 18m 40
S - 18m 60
S - 18m 40
S - 18m 20
S - 18m 00
S - 18m 10
S - 21m 00
S - 21m 80

Efforts suivant la direction des barres

Courbe des efforts tranchants

Courbe des moments fléchissants dus au vent

200

216

258

1 480 000

Moment de renversement

FIG. 21.

Driving the first rivet, October 24, 1881. One of Liberty's feet was brought out into the courtyard for the symbolic act, performed by Levi P. Morton, U.S. Minister to France. The assembling would be completed in the spring of 1884. *Library of Congress.*

The photographs on the following four pages document various stages in the construction of the statue and its skeleton. *Bartholdi Museum, in Colmar, and the Société Miège et Buhler, in Paris.*

A REVOLUTIONARY TECHNIQUE

On the outside of each full-sized plaster section, Bartholdi and his team built strong wooden molds, inside which the one-eighth-inch-thick sheets of copper that would form the final statue were hammered into shape. The carpentry work involved in making the molds was as complicated as forging casts in a foundry. Smaller or larger according to the complexity of the piece, the molds were constructed so that they could be easily detached from the plaster model and, later, from the copper. After the copper pieces were bent and shaped, they were turned in at the edges so that when put together, the joints would be invisible. Each piece was an average of four-and-one-half feet wide and thirty-two square feet in surface area, and to attach two pieces it was often necessary to join several molds. Sections with more complicated shapes sometimes had to be heated in the forge or joined with a soldering iron.

The completed copper sections were fitted on the inside with iron straps designed to give them rigidity. Forged to follow the curve of each piece, the iron straps were temporarily attached with screws. They would not be permanently fixed until the final assembling in America, when they were put in place with countersunk rivets invisible from the outside. It was these reinforcing iron straps that would be attached to the armature.

From the masonry base on which the statue would appear to rest, four immense angle-iron corner posts rose vertically, forming a central pylon nearly one hundred feet tall. Horizontal struts and crisscrossing diagonal bracing on each of the four sides assured its rigidity. Each corner post of the pylon was attached to the base with three huge bolts five-and-a-half inches in diameter secured sixty feet down inside the pedestal.

The system joining the copper sheets of the skin to the central pylon relied on a secondary flexible trusswork extending out from the pylon toward the skin. Each piece of copper hung separately, attached to the trusswork by thin iron bars fastened at each end with a single bolt. This was Eiffel's genius, providing the colossal statue with the necessary suppleness. Because of the extreme elasticity of the support system and the skin, the inevitable expansions and contractions of the metal in wind and weather were of little concern.

(continued)

(continued)

There remained a more difficult problem: corrosion. The wind from the sea always brings salt spray, which is extremely damaging to copper in combination with iron. With its copper skin and iron armature, the Statue of Liberty was potentially the greatest galvanic battery ever known. In Paris, the risk was not great, but New York Harbor was another matter. Therefore, as Liberty was assembled, French engineers placed pieces of copper wrapped in fabric that had been treated with anticorrosive minium (red lead) at the points where the skin touched the armature.

It was lucky for Bartholdi in that euphoric moment that he did not have the gift of long-range prophecy. The statue still had a long way to go. Just how long is indicated by what happened to the hand and torch when the Philadelphia Exposition closed. They were moved to the northwest corner of Madison Square in New York, on the theory that they would keep public interest alive during the short time before they had to be shipped back to France to be attached to the completed work. In 1880, four years later, they were still there, familiar and more or less forgotten. A newspaper joked about how children asked "embarrassing questions" when they saw it, and "nursemaids and grandmothers hardly [knew] how to answer."

The hard facts of life were that in both the United States and France it was hard to maintain the momentum of subscriptions. The French Committee kept working gallantly. In August 1877 they displayed a diorama in the gardens of the Tuileries showing the statue standing in the midst of New York's harbor. When the touring former President Grant came to Paris and visited the diorama in November, the event got a satisfying amount of press attention. Bartholdi helped, too, by waiving his copyright fees on 200 four-foot terra-cotta reproductions of the statue that the Committee sold in France. There was just enough money to keep some work on the statue going on in the workshops on the rue de Chazelles, but never enough to give the secure feeling that completion could be guaranteed.

Nonetheless, Bartholdi pushed on to the next phase, getting the head and shoulders ready to display at the Paris Universal Exposition scheduled for the summer of 1878. On June 28 of that year he had the new section ready. It was placed in a huge wagon, drawn by many horses, and hauled across the city to the Exposition grounds in the Champ de Mars, on the left bank of the Seine. At last people could see Liberty's face, and the effect was powerful. As the "fantastic, colossal head" passed down the boulevards and was silhouetted in the opening of the Arc de Triomphe, excited onlookers shouted "Vive la République!" One reporter took note of something "both curious and gracious" about Liberty's passage: "The bust is resting on a thick pile of branches, and at every turn in the route it sways a little, which gives it the air of nodding in salute to the curious crowd swarming around it. The effect is imposing; in spite of oneself one raises his hat to return the courtesy."

The bust was set up in front of the Pavilion of Nations with due ceremony, including the playing of the *Marseillaise*. However, in spite of praise from many visiting dignitaries, by the end of the Exposition the bust passed from being a novelty to an object of polite curiosity, like the arm and the torch still standing in New York. And the total sum of money necessary to see the job through was still not collected.

Undaunted, Bartholdi started work on the body of the giant. But in 1879, Viollet-le-Duc suddenly died, without leaving a plan for the skeleton.

To replace Viollet-le-Duc, Bartholdi turned to the only engineer in Paris who could meet the tremendous challenge of designing an interior framework that could carry the statue's weight and also steady it against the tremendous buffeting forces that would be exerted by Atlantic storms lashing New York's shores, blasting its thousands of square feet of thin copper surface with gale-force winds.

Gustave Eiffel was exactly the right choice. While Viollet-le-Duc's few ideas had been heavy and old-fashioned, Eiffel was already thinking in terms of twentieth-century technology. His specialty was the creation of metallic structures—such as the Garabit railroad bridge and, later, his world-famous Eiffel Tower—that were so light they seemed ready to fly, yet were enormously sturdy. Eiffel achieved this result by using cross-braced supporting trusses that evenly distributed the weight they carried in accordance with calculations of the utmost precision. Eiffel's works were poetic combinations of mathematics, technology, and art. He was originally trained as a chemist, and then went into iron-making before he found his vocation in engineering. He would live until 1923, and, not surprisingly, become a pioneer in the science of aerodynamics.

Traditional hollow statues—even one as big as the *San Carlo Borromeo*—usually had a solid armature of iron, wood, or masonry. That was impossible for the mammoth Statue of Liberty. What Eiffel gave it instead was a central tower, or pylon, made of wrought-iron plates connected together to form four immense girders, almost ninety-eight feet high. These were angled slightly toward each other in

French President Grévy visits Gaget's studio as the work progresses. *Le Journal Illustré, May 13, 1883. Private Collection, Paris.*

A doorway in the foot opened into the interior of the colossus. *Harper's Weekly, January 19, 1884. American Library in Paris.*

pyramidal form, and then connected by horizontal and diagonal bracing struts to form a rigid unit that carried the weight of the statue. To the upper part of the pylon Eiffel attached a smaller, similar structure of cross-braced girders as the core of the sixty-foot-long upraised arm.

From the pylon a light, open secondary framework looking something like a gigantic jungle gym reached out to connect with the skin of copper plates riveted together. But the actual connection was not direct. Instead, hundreds of thin, flat iron bars were attached at one end to the secondary framework, and to a webbing of metal straps on the inside of the copper plates at the other. These flexible connecting bars could expand, contract, and even bend and pivot slightly. They were, in effect, springs. Liberty's skin could breathe in heat and cold, and adapt itself to the changing forces of the wind. The combination of the powerful, rigid pylon and the flexible skin, joined by the lightweight framework and bars, was a work of genius. Unfortunately for the millions of visitors to the statue, its delicate structural brilliance is appreciable only to a trained eye when seen from inside the statue.

It took Eiffel all of 1880 to design this 120-ton framework. Like Bartholdi, he had no lack of self-confidence. When asked how long his creation could really expect to stand up to the repeated violence of nature, he replied with majestic simplicity: "It will hold."

While Bartholdi and Eiffel were hard at work, the Committee of the Franco-American Union mobilized itself for a final push to get more money. As late as midsummer of 1879 they were still 200,000 francs short. To raise the balance, they got permission from the Ministry of the Interior to conduct a national lottery. Though there were some attractive prizes, including a $4,000 table service, the receipts came in slowly, and the final drawing had to be rescheduled from December 1879 to June 1880. But at last the goal was reached. On July 7 the Committee proudly announced that, almost five years after the initial appeal, the subscription drive had taken in the necessary 600,000 francs. Nothing short of an act of God could now prevent completion of the work.

By the autumn of 1881, Bartholdi had completed many of the copper plates for the body, and Eiffel began to put up his pylon in the courtyard of the Gaget, Gauthier establishment. The twenty-fourth of October was the hundredth anniversary of the Battle of Yorktown, won by French and American arms, and it became the occasion for the first of the many ceremonies that would punctuate the long process of bringing the Statue of Liberty to America.

The ceremony on that October day was the driving of the first rivet for the complete assembly, and the honor went to the new American ambassador to France, Levi P. Morton, a New York banker who would later become Vice-President. One of the statue's feet was brought out and placed under the pylon, which was still only about one-fifth completed. An audience of two hundred was present, including Bartholdi, the management and work force of Gaget, Gauthier, and de Lesseps and other French and American notables. In a sense, the French guests of honor were Laboulaye and his close co-worker in the Union, Henri Martin, both of whom had recently been elected to the Senate of France.

The occasion was something of a last hurrah for these two liberal republicans. They both died in 1882. Under Laboulaye the Union had been an organization of high-minded, public-spirited private citizens, proud to be known as what we sometimes now call "do-gooders." But after Laboulaye's death, the French government took a much stronger interest in completing the statue. It became something of an affair of state, an official project blessed by the ministers of government.

With the money finally raised, the work of the Committee was essentially to supervise and publicize the final stages, which they pushed forward briskly. The pylon rose steadily to its full height of nearly one hundred feet, where it stood well above the roofs of the neighboring buildings. Below it, as a magazine in 1882 reported, "everyone was busy; amidst the noise of hammers and the heat of the forges, it was in every respect like the dissection, by sixty human beings, of an inhabitant of Brobdingnag." The torch was reclaimed from New York, and the colossus continued to rise until, by early 1884, *Liberty Enlightening the World* loomed majestically, even surrealistically, above the roofs of the seventeenth arrondissement.

The government of France's Third Republic let Ambassador Morton know that it was now fully involved in the work of the Franco-American Union, and would provide a warship to transport the statue to New York. It proposed to formally transfer the ownership of the statue to the United States government on July 4, 1884. Morton was somewhat perplexed. The project had begun as a people-to-people, not a government-to-government, affair; there was still no official American commitment to accept and take custody of the statue, and there was no certainty about the pedestal. He wrote hurriedly for instructions, and four days before the planned presentation he got a wire authorizing him to take part in the ceremonies as the representative of the President of the United States. He would accept the gift and thank the French people and the Franco-American Union, using his own discretion as to the exact words.

So the great day arrived. Once more the courtyard of Gaget, Gauthier and Company was gaily bedecked with flags and equipped with a speakers' platform. Once more a distinguished gathering crowded around the feet of the statue. Once more a band played the *Marseillaise* and the *Star-Spangled Banner*. De Lesseps, who had taken Laboulaye's place as head of the Union, and Morton arrived promptly at 11:30 A.M. and made their speeches, proffering and accepting the gift. Then, French bureaucracy being what it was, a formal report of the proceedings was passed around to be signed by all of the officials involved. Using a goose quill decorated with ribbons in the colors of both nations, they filled the page completely, leaving only a tiny space for the signature of the Prime Minister.

The colossus dwarfed the crowd, and a reporter observed that the United States flag, which was run up to float from the torch after the transfer, looked like a miniature ornament on a wedding cake. If anything, he said, could have moved the impassive features of Liberty, "it would be the thought of being 'handed over' from one to another of the tribes of pygmies gathered around her feet."

Then a select group, led by Bartholdi, entered the body through the open sole of the foot and began to climb the double-spiral staircase inside, in the dim light furnished by the sun shining through still-open

Opposite:

Above the rooftops. Liberty and her scaffolding dominate the skyline in this street scene painted in 1884 by Victor Dargaud. *Musée Carnavalet, Paris.*

To the New World. The French ship of war *Isère* carries the statue, packed in crates, to the United States in this painting by P. Adam, 1886. *Bartholdi Museum, Colmar.*

rivet holes. Only a few were sturdy enough to reach the top, among them the President of the Chamber of Deputies. He surveyed Paris from the crown, and then came down and restored himself after this physical exertion by hearty attention to the buffet. Gradually the guests left, many of them to meet again that night at the official celebration of Independence Day that would be given at the American Embassy.

And Liberty was left alone to gaze on the city of her birth.

Exactly at the moment when she officially became an American, the statue also became a stellar Paris attraction. It remained on display for the balance of the year, and the omnibuses passing through the neighborhood were always jammed. The transit company happily planned extra runs to accommodate everyone. The 112-foot-high woman (151 feet counting the upraised torch) was the talk of the town. The disassembly had been originally set for August 20, but was postponed for four months, much to the relief of those who had been unable to see the statue before it left for America.

In December, the lengthy operation of getting Liberty ready for the transatlantic voyage began. Taken down, labeled, and numbered, the pieces were organized into more than two hundred wooden chests and taken in wagons to a Paris rail terminal where a seventy-car train waited to carry them to Rouen, near the mouth of the Seine.[7] On May 21, 1885, in a pelting rain, and after more speeches and ceremonies, the French ship *Isère*, with the packing cases on board, and her escort vessel, the *Flore*, weighed anchor. The colors of France and America flew from the masts. Bartholdi was on deck to shepherd his "big girl" on the

Flags flying, the *Isère* arrives in New York, escorted by the frigate *Flore*. This photograph was taken from Bedloe's Island. *Musée National des Techniques, Paris.*

first few miles of her journey. He disembarked before the *Isère* reached the open sea, and Liberty sailed on alone toward her adopted land.

On June 17, the two French ships arrived and moored in the lower bay of New York's harbor, a few miles below the city. Two days later, under a brilliant sun, the *Isère* proceeded to Bedloe's Island for the unloading. Her black-and-gold lifeboats and the colorful pennants fluttering from the shrouds accentuated the spotless whiteness of her sleek hull. Four American naval vessels, carrying the mayor of New York and other notables, led the way. Small craft and steamboats crowded around. Band music, steam whistles, saluting cannon, and cheering crowds on the Battery created a constant uproar. Small boats took the American officials and the French officers to the tip of Manhattan, from where they rode up Broadway to a reception at City Hall.

It was a gala day, thanks to abundant newspaper publicity that had sharpened public interest by promising that the event would be spectacular. There was only one problem. The pedestal was not finished. Until only a few weeks earlier, it had looked as if it might never be. The American fund-raising effort had failed to come up with the needed cash and the Committee had given serious thought to not sending the statue over. Only the last-minute fund-raising exertions of Joseph Pulitzer, publisher of the New York *World*, convinced the members to change their minds.

It was all part of a dispiriting story. The American friends of the statue had committed themselves to building the pedestal in 1877. But eight years later—almost until the *Isère* was on the high seas—it was not certain that they would actually do it.

TOWARD THE NEW WORLD
76

CHAPTER THREE

TOWARD THE NEW WORLD

T he job of the American counterpart of the Franco-
American Union was to provide a home for Liberty,
a responsibility that was a neat metaphor for what the United States itself was supposed to do in the world.
But in both the literal and figurative senses, the job was never easy.

Things began well at the start of 1877. The American Committee for the Statue of Liberty created five
subcommittees, each with a well-defined charge. One was to prepare a general public appeal for funds.
Three others were to work specifically on press contacts, on any legislation that might be necessary, and
on winning the cooperation of organizations such as boards of trade and chambers of commerce. A final
subcommittee had the artistic assignment of selecting an artist and a design for the pedestal.

The legislative liaison group did its work effectively, and in a few weeks had secured the joint
congressional resolution that made either Bedloe's Island or Governor's Island available for the statue.
Both were federal property on which fortresses had been built early in the century as part of the harbor
defenses of New York. The joint resolution left the option of which one of the obsolete fortresses it would
give up in the hands of the administration.

Bartholdi much preferred Bedloe's. He thought its compact size and particular placement in the bay,
framed by New York, Brooklyn, and Jersey City, made it the perfect spot. Formerly owned by a New
Yorker named Isaac Bedloe, it had been bought by the federal government and used not only by the Army,
but also as a quarantine station where travelers with contagious illnesses could be isolated. There was a
small graveyard on the island containing the bodies of some soldiers and civilians who had died there. In
addition to the island's excellent location, Fort Wood, its aging garrison, had a stone wall in the shape of a
many-pointed star, surrounding a level parade ground—features which made it an ideal base for
Bartholdi's colossus.

Very shortly after the joint resolution was signed, General William Tecumseh Sherman, the Command-
ing General of the United States Army, personally inspected the harbor and, to Bartholdi's delight,
confirmed Bedloe's as the best site.

All seemed to be going well in the spring of 1877 when the pedestal subcommittee sent one of its
members over to Paris to solicit Bartholdi's ideas on the subject. As always, Bartholdi had firm ideas. Like
the statue, the pedestal and its elements must be unified by a "bold and clear design." There should be no
"multiplication of details" that would "destroy the proportions of the work."

Bartholdi had actually made a drawing, in 1875, of the statue on a pedestal that probably reflected
Viollet-le-Duc's taste for the medieval. It was a hexagonal turret that looked like a gigantic chess rook,
except that it had a row of arches around the top. It seemed to spring straight up from the fortress like a
giant stem.

This proposed design reflected an early mistake of Bartholdi's in thinking of the pedestal as a separate
composition, apart from the towering, vertical statue and the low, horizontal lines of the fortress at the
base. Three years later he suggested another plan to the pedestal subcommittee. This drawing showed a
supporting structure broken into two elements. From the fortress there would rise a great, stepped

William M. Evarts, President of
the American Committee. *Private
Collection, Paris.*

Opposite:

As the *Isère* arrives at Bedloe's
Island, crowds cheer the ship and
its precious cargo. In the foreground
is the pedestal still under construction. *L'Illustration, July 11, 1885.
Bibliothèque Forney, Paris.*

pyramid, surrounded by a low, decorated wall truncated near the top. On this flat base a simple, low, classical pedestal would stand. There would be a harmonious transition from the low, spread-out fortress to the statue, and the pedestal, though impressive, would be small enough to not detract attention from it.

Bartholdi passed these ideas on to be transmitted to whatever architect the Americans selected to do the pedestal. He assumed that while he worked steadily to finish the statue in Paris, there would be matching exertions in New York to prepare its perch.

But after the brave beginnings of 1877, this simply did not happen. The American Committee, however well intentioned, could make little headway against massive American indifference. Subscriptions were scarce. From time to time the press launched invocations of the memories of Lafayette and Washington and made fresh appeals to American generosity. Nothing seemed to work very well.

The last years of the 1870s were not a particularly good time for the American Committee's appeals. The country's energies, already stretched by the economic depression of 1873, were focused on the settlement of the West and the rise of large urban areas and their attendant problems. The aggressive growth of industry and the procession of exciting inventions held more interest for Americans than did public statuary. The days of Washington and Lafayette seemed as remote as ancient history.

And there was more, too. Then as now, New York was sometimes resented by other parts of the country. It was seen with considerable justification as the home of the great trusts, the powerful banks, the gamblers on the stock market, the arrogant millionaire industrialists and magnates who made life difficult for the worker, the farmer, and the middling-sized merchant. Hence, many Americans living outside the city were left cold by requests for money to build a mighty monument in New York. "Let New York pay for it," was their attitude, and they were also skeptical about a "gift" that required the recipients to dig deeply into their own pockets to create a setting for it. And the Committee (whose most prominent members were New Yorkers) did a poor job of answering such objections. They were not able to explain the universal significance of Liberty as a symbol and the special nature of the statue as a unique gift from the people of one nation to those of another.

TOWARD THE NEW WORLD

By 1881, virtually nothing had been done on the American side. But then the commemorations of the hundredth anniversary of the Battle of Yorktown rekindled some public interest in the memorial, and the news that the Franco-American Union had completed its fund raising spurred Evarts to see for himself how things were going in Paris. Inspired by how far along the statue had progressed, he wrote Richard Butler, the secretary of the American Committee, saying that he was "greatly impressed by the happy fashion in which Bartholdi had carried out his noble conception." The American Committee must move with "promptness and energy" to provide for the pedestal that would receive this "contribution of French genius, friendship and enthusiasm."

Galvanized into a fresh burst of activity, the Committee named an architect, and established an estimate of costs and completion time for the pedestal—$250,000 and nine months.[1]

The architect was Richard Morris Hunt, an excellent choice with a special feeling for French sculpture. Born in 1828 to a prosperous New England family, he had studied at the Ecole des Beaux-Arts in Paris, and was its first American graduate. He knew Viollet-le-Duc and had taken part in designing some parts of a major renovation of the Louvre. When Hunt returned to New York after the Civil War he became a successful society architect, building sumptuous town houses in New York and palatial summer "cottages" at Newport for rich clients. But he dreamed of projects that would allow him a somewhat wider wingspread, for which he had ample talent.

Hunt spent more than a year thinking about the right design for the pedestal, and his first draft was a version of Bartholdi's pyramid. He lowered it and made it a broad platform of inclined planes rising above the fortress wall, with a staircase in the center of each side. That was just the base on which the pedestal would rest. The pedestal itself would be 114 feet high and slightly tapered. The ornamentation would consist of blocks of stone, with some projecting, in a checkerboard pattern, a pair of cornices, and a triple loggia on each side.

The American Committee, which could sense a big architect's bill in the offing, forced Hunt to modify his design. He cut the pedestal to eighty-nine feet but then increased some of the ornamentation to harmonize better with the new proportions. In the end, no money was saved.

The American Committee felt a sense of urgency about getting something accomplished, and work on setting the foundation began in 1883 even though Hunt was still working on his preliminary studies. The foundation stone was to be of concrete, and setting it was an immense undertaking. The Committee made another good choice in putting the work under the supervision of General Charles Pomeroy Stone, who had trained at West Point as an engineer. Stone had had an unlucky Civil War record[2] and resigned from the Army in 1864 to work for a mining corporation. In 1870 he went to Egypt to become the chief of staff of its army, at the invitation of Ismail Pasha—the same Khedive for whom Bartholdi had once hoped to build "Progress Bringing the Light to Asia."

Stone was a good organizer and an energetic worker. Starting in April of 1883, he turned Bedloe's Island into a huge campsite where more than a hundred men were quartered. Crews first dug a giant excavation in Fort Wood's parade ground—big enough to hold what would be the largest slab of concrete ever poured into a single block. The pouring began in October and went on, layer by layer, through the harsh winter. Ground level was not reached until the following March. Stone's workmen continued to pour and finished the foundation in June. It stood fifty-two feet above the parade ground and had swallowed up 24,000 barrels of Portland cement and great quantities of traprock and water, along with most of the funds thus far collected in the United States.

The Committee had been struggling for money all through 1883. It sent special solicitors, district by district, into New York's factories, workshops, and offices begging for cash. It sponsored art fairs and benefit shows and lectures, and sold miniatures of the statue and even copies of Bartholdi's autograph. It seized on every opportunity for publicity, such as the occasion on which a little girl sent in a small

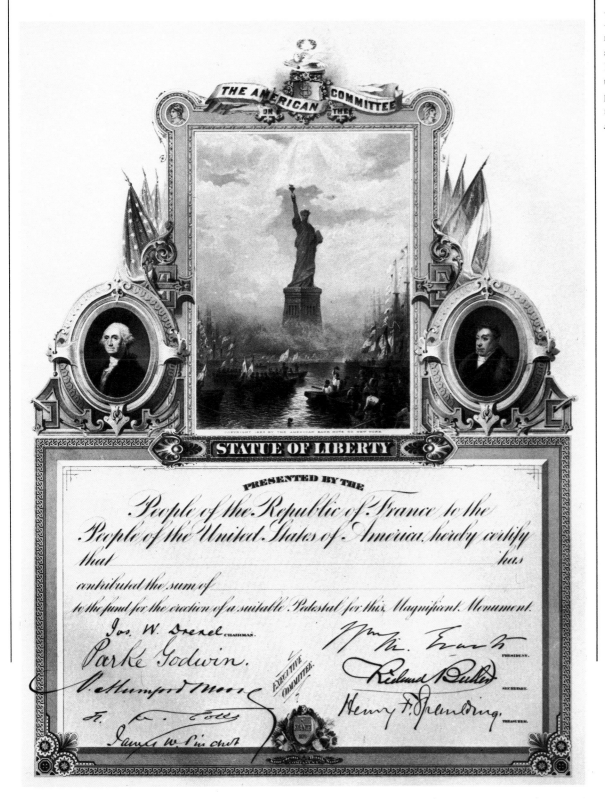

Donors to the pedestal fund received a handsome certificate of appreciation, which reproduced Edward Moran's romantic vision of the statue in New York Harbor—painted three years before the monument was unveiled. *Bartholdi Museum, Colmar.*

Plan and profile of the armature showing how the pylon would attach to the pedestal. *Scientific American, June 13, 1885. Bibliothèque du Conservatoire National des Arts et Métiers, Paris.*

Top right:

R. M. Hunt's 1883 design represents a midway point in the evolution of the pedestal's form. Hunt had seen that Bartholdi's own conception, a massive pyramidal structure that looked fine on paper, would appear too squat and ungainly atop the broad bastions of star-shaped Fort Wood. Hunt opted instead for a towerlike structure whose upward thrust would counterbalance the horizontal lines of the fort. One hundred and fourteen feet tall, Hunt's design nevertheless threatened to dwarf Bartholdi's statue. This consideration, together with rapidly disappearing funds, brought the height down to eighty-nine feet. The final pedestal kept the four-columned loggias on each side of Hunt's design, as well as the frieze of forty shields symbolizing the forty states of the Union at the time. *The American Institute of Architects Foundation, Washington, D.C.*

Bottom right:

The pedestal would rise from a massive concrete foundation, still encased in its wooden forms. *Harper's Weekly, July 12, 1884. American Library in Paris.*

Opposite:

Hunt's final design for the pedestal. *Collection of Ernest Chambré, New York.*

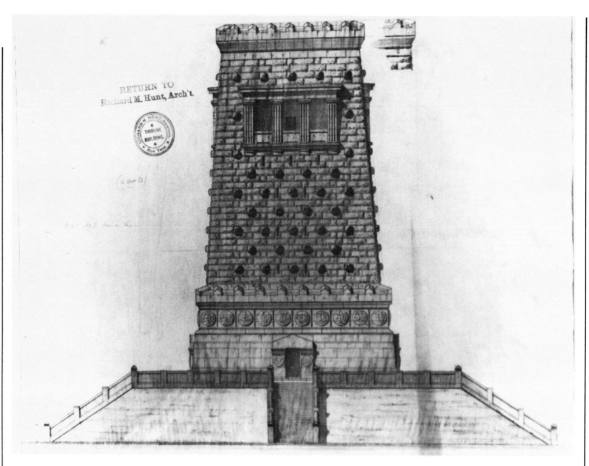

contribution accompanied by a letter suggesting that a penny be asked from every schoolchild in the country. Newspaper coverage of the story created a touching legend of little ones donating their candy money, but in fact the idea brought in very little. Desperately, the Committee used its political influence to get the New York State legislature to authorize New York City to make a gift of $50,000. But the fiscally conservative governor of New York, Grover Cleveland, vetoed the bill. Two years later, as President of the United States, Cleveland would preside at the inauguration of the statue.

As of July 4, 1884, when Liberty was formally handed over to the United States, the Committee's bank account held $20,000, barely enough to lay two or three rows of the stones in the pedestal. Sarcastic cartoons in the press showed Liberty as a wrinkled old crone, still waiting for her platform.

The Committee leaders knew that if the project was not to collapse entirely in ridicule they had to at least give the appearance of pushing resolutely ahead. So plans were announced to lay the first stone of the

WILLIAM A. BRODIE, THE GRAND MASTER

Right:

The Masonic ceremony of laying the first stone took place on August 5, 1884, under steady rain. *Harper's Weekly, August 16, 1884. American Library in Paris.*

Five hundred spectators watched the proceedings from beneath their umbrellas. *Frank Leslie's Illustrated Newspaper, August 16, 1884. Private Collection, Paris.*

pedestal on August 5. Presumably in deference to Bartholdi's membership in the Masonic brotherhood, the organization of the ceremonies was put in the hands of R.W. (Reverend Worshipful) Franck R. Lawrence, Deputy Grand Master of the Grand Lodge of the State of New York.

The Committee had hoped for a grand public relations spectacle, but on the appointed day the weather added to the troubles that had dogged the pedestal project. A record downpour soaked the five hundred guests who gathered at the foot of Broadway to make up a procession down to the Battery. Showing no respect to the assortment of senators, representatives, mayors, governors, generals, consuls, and ambassadors, the torrential rains poured down on them as they crossed the bay, made their way up dripping steps, and huddled under umbrellas on the flat, sixty-seven-foot-square top of the concrete foundation.

Soggy French and American flags and limp pennants on small boats around the island made a pathetic attempt to lend a holiday air. A derrick held the cornerstone of the pedestal, suspended by cables, ready to be lowered and cemented in place by a silver trowel[3]. After the customary benediction, a kind of time capsule, a copper chest containing current newspapers, calling cards of visiting officials, and medals and coins struck in honor of the occasion, was sealed and put in a hollow spot under the cornerstone, which was then lowered into place. Deputy Grand Master Lawrence then solemnly declared the cornerstone "plumb, level and square," cemented it, tapped it three times with a mallet, and announced that it was duly laid. Then wheat, wine, and oil were sprinkled over it.

There were speeches in spite of the rain, followed by a chorus of *Old Hundred*, and a twenty-one-gun salute from cannon on the esplanade of the fort. The ceremony was, in fact, very moving and as one reporter observed, gave the occasion a broad dimension. It reminded the spectators of the hope that Liberty offered to future generations—"a state of peace, respect and justice."

The mood was broken as the guests came down off the platform and scrambled through the mud to the dock for the return trip. One paper the next day said they would have been less wet if they had swum back to the Battery.

The Committee struggled through the next seven months to little avail. Money trickled in from odd sources—veterans' and patriotic groups, civic clubs, philanthropic societies. In eight years the Committee had managed to raise a total of $182,491.40—only $10,000 of it from outside New York. But by March 1885 they had spent $179,625.41. The American Committee for the Statue of Liberty had only $2,885.99 left and was running out of ideas. During the winter they had turned, as a last resort, to their friends in Congress and petitioned for a Joint Resolution that would give them $100,000 to carry on. They waited anxiously to see if the federal Treasury would bail them out. The decision fell like an axe: No.

Hunt's design was already completed, calling for the delivery of hundreds of huge blocks of granite, and arrangements had been made to bring them in from Leeds Island, off the shore of Connecticut. Now they lay useless on the docks, awaiting shipment.[4] There was not enough in the till to pay for the blocks or to pay the workmen to put them in place. Evarts, Butler, and General Stone had no choice. They ordered work stopped on March 10.

At the moment the Statue of Liberty was being packed for its voyage, the pedestal was nonexistent. The Franco-American Union's Committee in Paris was hesitant, under the circumstances, about whether or not it should send the statue over. The American part of the joint effort had simply collapsed.

It was at this point that Liberty's savior appeared on the scene. For all of the hard work by committees, the story of how the statue was built, against the odds, is largely an account of determined, talented individuals with strong convictions. Laboulaye. Bartholdi. Eiffel.

And now, Joseph Pulitzer. Pulitzer was a classic American success story, the living proof of what a man of talent and fire could accomplish under liberty. He had come to the United States as a skinny and penniless Hungarian immigrant in 1864. After serving in the Union army in the Civil War he settled in St. Louis where he quickly made himself a popular figure and political broker in the large German-speaking community there. He married well, bought a newspaper, the *Post-Dispatch*, and made it thrive. In August 1883 he looked for greener pastures in America's biggest city. Moving to New York, he bought a moribund little paper, the *World*, with an eye to reviving it.

Joseph Pulitzer, publisher of the New York *World*, painted in 1905 by John Singer Sargent. *Collection of Joseph Pulitzer, Jr., St. Louis, Missouri.*

The names of new subscribers appeared every day in the *World* beneath this cut of Uncle Sam and Liberty. *The New York World, May 18, 1885. Private Collection, Paris.*

Construction resumed each time new dollars poured into the fund. *Harper's Weekly, June 6, 1885. American Library in Paris.*

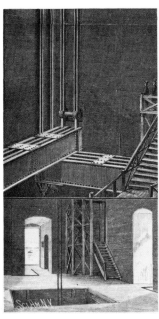

Opposite:

A steam-powered derrick lifts materials to the workers. *Frank Leslie's Illustrated Newspaper, August 21, 1886. Private Collection, Paris.*

Left:

Men at work inside Liberty's head, attaching the copper sheets to the ironwork skeleton. *Frank Leslie's Illustrated Newspaper, October 23, 1886. Private Collection, Paris.*

Bottom left:

The elevator shaft and the girders anchoring the statue to the pedestal. *Scientific American, August 14, 1886. American Library in Paris.*

Bottom right:

The assembling begins: thin, flat iron bars attach the foot and part of the dress to the armature. *Scientific American, August 14, 1886. American Library in Paris.*

In closeup, Liberty's features appear formidable. *Private Collection, Paris.*

Opposite:

Hurrying to finish, workers swarm over the statue preparing to raise the face into position. *L'Illustration, October 23, 1886. Bibliothèque Forney, Paris.*

Red-bearded, furiously active, and opinionated, Pulitzer knew that the secret of success for a modern journal aimed at a mass audience was first to entertain, then to counsel and inform its readers. A Pulitzer paper gave its readers the very best and latest in journalistic technology, but, above all, it was their friend. The *World* was sprightly, nosy, and innovative. It ran the first comic strips. It had some of the earliest investigative reporters. One of them was Elizabeth Cochrane, who wrote spirited columns under the pen name "Nelly Bly." Pulitzer once sent her around the world in eighty days to prove the wonders of modern transportation. Although Pulitzer rapidly became a millionaire himself, his editorial page was forever announcing it was on the side of the people against the fat cats and the crooked politicians. Pulitzer gave the age of steam and steel a voice of brass.

He thrived on causes. And in 1883, he discovered a sensational cause in the failure of upper-crust New York to provide the $250,000 for the Statue of Liberty pedestal. He wrote: "Here in the commercial metropolis of the Western world, where hundreds of our citizens reckon their wealth by millions, where our merchants and bankers and brokers are spoken of as 'princes,' we stand haggling and begging and scheming in order to raise enough money to procure a pedestal on which to place the statue.... The dash of one millionaire merchant's pen ought to settle the matter and spare the city further information...."

On March 15, 1885, when the sorry state of the Committee's finances became front-page news, Pulitzer moved into high journalistic gear: "It would be an irrevocable disgrace to New York City and the American republic to have France send us this splendid gift without our having provided even so much as a landing place for it.... There is but one thing that can be done. *We* must raise the money. The *World* is the people's paper, and it now appeals to the people to come forward and raise the money. The $250,000 that the making of the Statue cost was paid in by the masses of the French people—by the working men, the tradesmen, the shopgirls, the artisans—by all, irrespective of class or condition. Let us respond in like manner. Let us not wait for the millionaires to give this money. It is not a gift from the millionaires of France to the millionaires of America, but a gift of the whole people of France to the whole people of America. Take this appeal to yourself personally.... Give something, however little.... Let us hear from the people."

The effect was electrifying and gave new life to the flagging subscription drive. Every week, under a cut showing Uncle Sam holding out his hat like a poor box in front of the statue, the paper printed a list of donors—each and every one, no matter how small the contribution. To see one's name in the paper, or to see whether one's friends were in it, was exactly the kind of thrill that kept readers putting down their daily pennies to buy the *World*. Every dollar Pulitzer made for the statue further strengthened his own fortune.

In just two months the *World* collected $52,203.41, more than a quarter of what it had taken the Committee seven years to gather. The work at Bedloe's Island began again. Pulitzer was boomingly confident that it was only the beginning, and his judgment was completely justified. The receipts kept growing and the *World*'s lists of small contributors from all over the country kept growing. By the time the statue actually arrived, in mid-June, most of the $100,000 the Committee still needed was in hand. By August some 120,000 subscribers had given $101,191. "The statue itself gains an inestimable value from this fact. It is not only an ideal of Liberty—but an attestation of Liberty in every stone—The people have done their work well—Their liberality has saved the great Republic from disgrace." And with a final flourish, the *World* handed over $100,000 to the Committee and spent the rest (a very generous sum in

October 28, 1886, the day of the official unveiling. As one observer remarked, it was more than a flotilla, it was an entire fleet that made its way to Bedloe's Island. *Bartholdi Museum, Colmar.*

Menu for a banquet given in Bartholdi's honor, November 18, 1885. *Bibliothèque du Conservatoire National des Arts et Métiers, Paris.*

Opposite:

"Homage to Bartholdi." *Judge* published this tribute to Bartholdi and Liberty's American supporters the week the statue was unveiled. *Judge, October 30, 1886. Private Collection, Paris.*

·Menu·

CHATEAU YQUEM	Huîtres
	Potages
	Consommé à la souveraine
AMONTILLADO	Tortue verte à la royale
Variés	Hors d'oeuvre Variés
	Timbales Lagardère
	Poisson
	Aiguillettes de bass à la Chitry
JOHANNISBERGER, Bbq Seal	Concombres
	Relevé
PERRIER-JOUET	Selle de chevreuil à l'Athalin
	Haricots panachés
	Entrée
ST. PIERRE	Terrapène à la Baltimore
	SORBET A L'ANDALOUSE
	Rôti
ROMANEE CONTI	Canvas-back duck
	Froid
	Aspic de foie-gras historié
	Entremets sucrés
PERRIER-JOUET	Poires à la Ferrière
Pièces montées	Glace fantaisie
	Dessert Fruits
LIQUEURS	Café
Le 18 Novembre 1885.	616 5TH AVE.

The city was transformed. The City Hall, the main Post Office, hotels and homes and clubs everywhere were bedecked with French and American colors, giving "to the physical aspect of the metropolis," said one newspaper story, "something analogous to the bright spirit of rejoicing that stirred in every human breast." The southernmost stretch of Broadway offered a view of uninterrupted rows of banners. Pulitzer, as usual, led all the rest in ostentation. He had a triumphal arch of greenery stretched across Park Row in front of the *World* building, with a large sign that read (in French): "La Belle France—the United States: Vive l'entente fraternelle des deux républiques." ("Long live the fraternal union of the two republics.")

Everything combined to make the day magnificent—except the weather. It had poured the night before, and when morning came the sky was like lead and the harbor mantled in fog so thick that the statue was invisible. Nonetheless, said one participant, "human joy has rarely been so bright." From daybreak crowds surged everywhere. "Not a square centimeter of the streets was clear," testified a foreign reporter. "The Brooklyn Bridge groans under its load of humanity. Sidewalks, portals, balconies, penthouses were covered by a happy throng." Pitchmen had a field day, shouting themselves hoarse, selling pictures and medallions and portraits of General Grant, some of which were passed off as portraits of de Lesseps, as well as whatever other knicknacks moldering in their shops could be spruced up to look like commemorative items.

The official reviewing stand was in Madison Square. The French delegation made its way there, escorted by one of the city's local militia units—naturally, the Lafayette Guards. Shortly after ten o'clock President Cleveland and his escort joined them after a carriage ride down from Fifty-seventh Street.

Then the impressive paraders, twenty thousand strong, swung by, stepping along Fifth Avenue and turning southward into Broadway down to the Battery. General Stone, the Grand Marshal, surrounded by

JUDGE'S COMPLIMENTS TO BARTHOLDI AND THE MONUMENT COMMITTEE.

An artillery salute welcomed President Cleveland to Bedloe's Island, and the resulting smoke nearly hid the statue from view. Photograph by H. O. Neil, October 28, 1886. *Library of Congress.*

Opposite, top:

At the summit: Twelve visitors at a time could view New York Harbor from the observation deck surrounding the torch. *L'Illustration, July 4, 1885. Bibliothèque Forney, Paris.*

Opposite, center:

The first steps inside the head: visitors brave the spiral staircase to take in the view through windows in Liberty's crown. *Le Monde Illustré, September 28, 1878. Bibliothèque Forney, Paris.*

Opposite, bottom:

Fireworks scheduled to take place the day of the unveiling had to be postponed because of rain, but all other festivities proceeded on schedule. *Harper's Weekly, November 6, 1886. American Library in Paris.*

Though Congress refused to appropriate money for liquor, champagne was available at the celebration. *Judge, October 30, 1886. Private Collection, Paris.*

ELITE-SEC CHAMPAGNE.

The *World*'s "Arc de Triomphe," constructed of greenery outside the newspaper's office. *The New York World, October 29, 1886. Private Collection, Paris.*

Opposite:

The statue at night, as imagined by the artist Edward Moran ten years before the unveiling. *Bartholdi Museum, Colmar.*

his staff and followed by the fanfare of the Marine Band, led the march. One after another, to the crashing beat of military marches, came federal soldiers, the New York National Guard, battalions of veterans, and grandiosely named volunteer regiments of infantry and cavalry—the Sons of Lafayette and Rochambeau, the Rochambeau Grenadiers, and the Washington Guard, escorting a coach that had been used by the Father of his Country. Each band tried to be heard above the others, and up and down the line the solid crowds heard the overlapping strains of *Hail Columbia*, the *Star-Spangled Banner*, *Yankee Doodle*, *Dixie*, and, over and over again, the *Marseillaise*.

Behind the military units came rank after rank of civilians, demonstrating the melting-pot nature of New York. There were Freemasons and civic clubs, student associations and philanthropic lodges. At least three culinary societies marched in the parade. Clubs of Frenchmen had the place of honor, including the Harmony Club, the Colmarian Society, the Alsace-Lorraine Union, and the Alsatian Union, all of them especially gratified to be honoring their compatriot, Bartholdi. The parade was closed out by the volunteer firemen, pulling along their gaily decorated machines.

The procession took more than three hours to pass the reviewing stand, and the President and party had to leave for the island before it concluded. Rain had begun to fall, but spirits were high as the marchers reached the Battery. Charles Bigot described the scene: "It is an extraordinary spectacle, and a pity that the rain keeps us from seeing it clearly. Ahead of us, behind us, all around is a flotilla, or rather an entire fleet, which is heading for Bedloe's Island. Everything that floats in New York, Brooklyn or Jersey City— steamers, ferry boats, yachts—has lit its boilers for this ceremony. All these boats are bedecked with colors…and all are crowded, to the point of being in danger of foundering, with an enthusiastic and joyous throng. It looks as if at this moment the entire population of the three cities is on the water. When we arrive off Bedloe's, a hundred, two hundred ships are already grouped round us, forming a kind of floating archipelago of crowded islands; and other ships never stop coming from everywhere."

When the President finally set foot on Bedloe's Island, where a band had been entertaining early arrivals, an uproar broke loose. Cannon boomed out, and every boat in the harbor with a steam whistle opened it full blast. Some of them, and some downtown buildings, were also equipped with sirens, which Bigot had never heard before and never wished to hear again. The sound, he said, was "simultaneously a whistling, a screeching, a roaring…it squeals like a saw, with a…noise which tears apart the eardrum." It looked innocuous on top of a boiler—a slim pipe with a slight bulge. "But let the steam escape through that pipe under a few atmospheres of pressure, and it sets a number of metal blades whirling…and this inoffensive-looking apparatus becomes immediately something terrible, formidable, frightful."

So many bells, sirens, and whistles were in constant use that only a few members of the audience could hear the well-respected Brooklyn preacher, the Reverend Richard Storrs, deliver the invocation. Next, de Lesseps made still another official presentation of the statue which loomed behind him, partly invisible in the thick haze, with a veil covering her face. Next it was Evarts's turn to respond on behalf of the American Committee. It had been arranged that the conclusion of his remarks would be the moment of unveiling. It is said to have been Bartholdi, who had been standing impatiently inside the head most of the afternoon, who held the cord that would release the veil; he kept his eye on a confederate at ground level who was supposed to wave to him when Evarts had finished speaking. Evarts, still going strong, took a lengthy pause for breath, and the nervous official mistakenly flashed the signal. The veil dropped and immediately every noisemaking device in the harbor, from cannon to human throats, let loose in an indescribable din. Evarts was no mean orator, and he gamely finished his remarks, but almost no one except President Cleveland heard him.

Finally the noise abated sufficiently for the public speaking to continue. President Cleveland received the statue on behalf of the United States, and Albert LeFaivre, Consul-General of France in New York, made an official response. Rain or no rain, no occasion in that more patient, speech-savoring era was complete without a formal commemorative oration, and on hand to deliver it was New York's best-liked after-dinner speaker, Chauncey M. Depew, attorney, railroad director, politician, socialite, and raconteur. He spoke at length, before yielding finally to the Reverend Henry C. Potter for the final benediction.

Light for Liberty. Even after the unveiling, financial problems remained, including the question of who would pay to light the statue. Thomas Nast's cartoon shows Liberty snuffed out. *Harper's Weekly, November 20, 1886. American Library in Paris.*

Opposite:

The Freedom of the City of New York (honorary citizenship) was conferred upon Auguste Bartholdi by the city on October 27, 1886, the day before the Statue of Liberty opened. *Bartholdi Museum, Colmar.*

Then, in great disarray, the dignitaries reembarked for Manhattan and the various evening festivities still ahead. At last, twenty-one years after the famous dinner at Glatigny, the idealistic project conceived that night was completed. *Liberty Enlightening the World*, now officially installed, lifted her torch above the waters of the New World.

The weather and the vicissitudes of government wiped out a final planned moment of glory. There was supposed to be a fireworks show when darkness fell. But the fog and rain made that impossible. And Liberty's light was supposed to shine forth as she made her debut as a beacon. That turned out to be a fiasco.

Bartholdi's early drawings had shown rays of light streaming from the crown. Whether this was in imitation of the lighthouse at Alexandria, or part of the program for getting Congress to grant the site of Bedloe's Island, is uncertain. The fact is that the United States authorities expected Liberty to be a lighthouse, and in 1885 Bartholdi offered an idea of how to make it work as one. The idea of searchlights in the head was long gone. Instead, he envisioned strong lamps placed around the edge of the platform of the torch. They would shine up and down, illuminating both the clouds and the waves, and be visible as a reference point from miles away.

In the months prior to the inauguration, the American Electric Company told the American Committee that it would furnish ten 8,000-candlepower lamps free, as well as the cables and installation—the equivalent of a $7,000 contribution. The Committee likewise made arrangements with E. P. Hampson and Company to furnish electric power for the first week—from October 28 to November 4—assuming that the United States would then pick up the bill and carry on financing the lighting from there.

One week before the inauguration, with the lamps already in place, however, trouble began. An Army lieutenant of engineers appeared on the scene, authorized by the Lighthouse Board to review and approve of the lighting plans. He decidedly did not approve of Bartholdi's idea. The rays shining upward, he said, would reflect off the clouds and be confusing to distant navigators. They should emerge horizontally from the torch. To achieve that, he had the lamps moved to the inside of the torch's flame, which he ordered pierced with two rows of bull's-eyes covered with thick glass.

Bartholdi tried to intervene, but the matter was out of his hands. He protested, as did electrical specialists, that the intense heat generated by the lights would, in their new location, ruin the copper of the flame. Moreover, the horizontally directed rays would light neither the statue nor the water. But the lieutenant did not listen. When the switch was thrown, only a feeble halo of barely visible light came from the torch. Bartholdi said it looked like a glowworm. For all practical purposes, when night came the statue was plunged in darkness. That was not all. On inauguration day, there was no sign of any official appropriation or authorization to pay for the necessary electric current. The Committee had no more funds to give. E. P. Hampson was going to be stuck if it kept its agreement to furnish power. Until the very last minute, the company kept trying to find someone in Washington who could guarantee them their money, but in vain. There was a wall of bureaucratic silence. Late in the afternoon, rather than embarrass the United States by refusing to turn on the current with the French visitors still present, Hampson agreed that it would make a gift of electricity until November 6, the day on which the Frenchmen would sail for home, but not a day longer. So honor was saved.

But the dream of Liberty literally enlightening the entrance to the New World was stillborn. And the government's management of the statue was off to a floundering start. Things would not improve very much. Various attempts to implement the lighthouse idea were fruitless. One of Bartholdi's suggestions was to cover the torch with gold or some bright, reflecting metal off which the light could bounce. But simply making the torch or the entire statue more visible at night was not enough for navigation purposes. Finally, in 1902, America resigned itself to the idea that the statue was purely a work of art, without the redeeming, utilitarian feature of being a beacon as well. It was transferred to the custody of the War Department because the Army engineers still had authority over structures in the harbor and no one in Washington could think of a better pigeonhole.

But that was only one of many transitions that Liberty Enlightening the World was undergoing as she entered on her new life as an American—and universal—symbol.

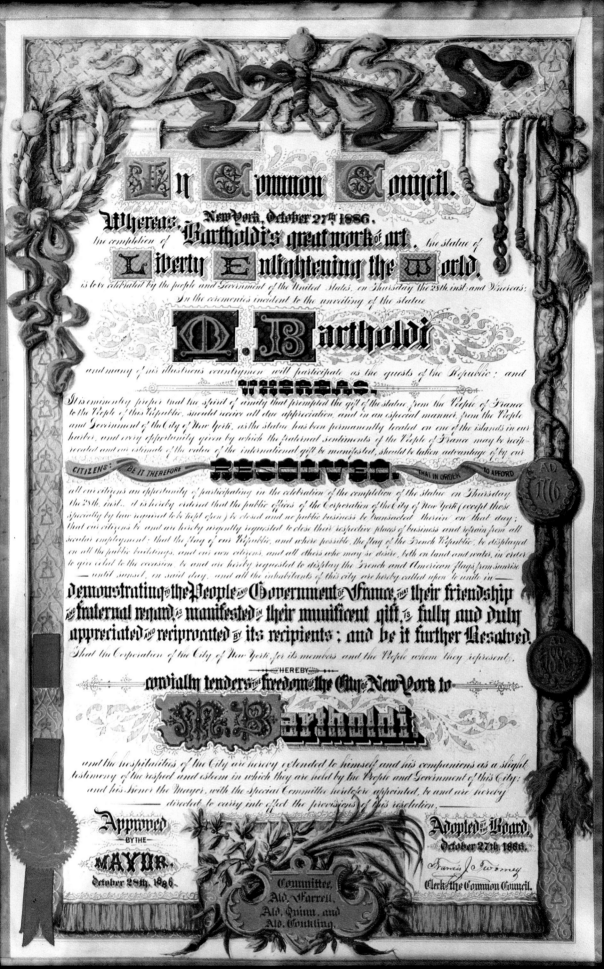

In Common Council.

Whereas, New York, October 27th 1886, the completion of Bartholdi's great work of art, the statue of

Liberty Enlightening the World,

is to be celebrated by the people and Government of the United States, on Thursday the 28th inst: and Whereas: In the ceremonies incident to the unveiling of the statue

M. Bartholdi

and many of his illustrious countrymen will participate as the guests of the Republic; and

WHEREAS,

It is eminently proper that the spirit of amity that prompted the gift of the statue from the People of France to the People of this Republic, should receive all due appreciation, and in an especial manner, from the People and Government of the City of New York, as the statue has been permanently located on one of the islands in our harbor, and every opportunity given by which the fraternal sentiments of the People of France may be reciprocated and our estimate of the value of the international gift be manifested, should be taken advantage of by our

CITIZENS': BE IT THEREFORE **RESOLVED,** THAT IN ORDER TO AFFORD

all our citizens an opportunity of participating in the celebration of the completion of the statue on Thursday, the 28th, inst.. it is hereby ordered that the public offices of the Corporation of the City of New York (except those specially by law required to be kept open) be closed and no public business be transacted therein on that day; that our citizens be and are hereby urgently requested to close their respective places of business and refrain from all secular employment; that the flag of our Republic, and where possible, the flag of the French Republic, be displayed on all the public buildings, and our own citizens, and all others who may so desire, both on land and water, in order to give eclat to the occasion be and are hereby requested to display the French and American flags from sunrise until sunset, in said day, and all the inhabitants of this city are hereby called upon to unite in

demonstrating to the People and Government of France, that their friendship and fraternal regard, as manifested in their munificent gift, is fully and duly appreciated and reciprocated by its recipients; and be it further Resolved,

That the Corporation of the City of New York, for its members and the People whom they represent, HEREBY

cordially tenders the freedom of the City of New York to

M. Bartholdi

and the hospitalities of the City are hereby extended to himself and his companions as a slight testimony of the respect and esteem in which they are held by the People and Government of this City; and his Honor the Mayor, with the special Committee heretofore appointed, be and are hereby directed to carry into effect the provisions of this resolution.

Approved BY THE **MAYOR.** October 28th, 1886.

Adopted BY THE BOARD, October 27th 1886.

Francis J. Twomey
Clerk of the Common Council.

Committee,
Ald. Farrell,
Ald. Quinn, and
Ald. Conkling.

CHAPTER FOUR

THE GOLDEN DOOR

America had not stood still in the twenty-one years between the dinner at Glatigny, when a monument was first proposed, and the day in New York when Liberty was finally dedicated. During the first decades of the statue's presence in the harbor, there would be even more transformation, bringing into being a modern United States that seemed to have little resemblance to the nation that Laboulaye and Bartholdi had wanted France to honor and to imitate. Would the statue keep its meaning in the face of such changes?

The eighteenth-century America of Franklin, Washington, Jefferson, and Madison was, for the most part, a collection of strong local communities that governed themselves and earned their livelihoods by farming and trade. To members of the educated elite in France and America, these communities looked enough like republican Rome or the free city-states of Greece to seem perfect nurseries of good citizenship and virtue as expounded by ancient writers. Dressed in its classical robes, the statue appeared to embody those civic ideals.

But some fifty-three years after the 1788 adoption of the Constitution, when Alexis de Tocqueville published the second volume of *Democracy in America*, the original pattern was already changing. The western boundary of the United States had been extended to the Rockies, and Americans predicted, correctly, that it was their "manifest destiny" to reach the Pacific within a few years. Steamboats were knitting this huge territory together, and the locomotive had just come on the scene. The telegraph was around the corner. Factories were producing shoes, textiles, flour, and meat. The population had jumped from four to almost twenty million, and large cities like New Orleans, Cincinnati, Philadelphia, New York, and Boston were already trying to cope with such urban problems as sanitation and crime. Mass popular voting had put a heavy dose of power in the hands of people without higher education or property.

Most Americans were still small-town and farm folk, and the gap between rich and poor was not a chasm. Men like Tocqueville and Laboulaye were sure that religion, literacy, and common interests would keep society from being split between mobs and aristocrats. Democracy, although tainted by slavery, was thriving in America and would be irresistible to the whole world. In romantic terms, they believed the spirit of Liberty was on the march in human affairs. With forward stride and uplifted torch, the statue's design seemed to fit *that* notion perfectly. As it took form in Bartholdi's models and sketches, it had become a combination of classical and romantic elements, ideally matched to America's essence.

In a sense the statue seemed to belong, as memorials do, to the past. Yet it could not be completely or exclusively identified with history and historical happenings. From the start, it belonged to the future. The revolutionary techniques used in its construction made it a perfect example of the progress that was worshiped by a future-oriented Western world. And all the speeches at the inaugural ceremonies evoked the feeling that Liberty was the hope of the world in times yet to come.

She did stand for Franco-American friendship in the American Revolution, but that was only one of her many messages. She was also to be the harbinger of an era of international peace.

She did stand for a classical definition of liberty, under law, and for social stability as against anarchy or tyranny. Certainly Laboulaye and the conservative American sponsors of the statue like Evarts, Cleve-

The Commerce of Nations Paying Homage to Liberty. Painting by Edward Moran, 1876. *Collection of Katharine D. Hellman, New York.*

land, and Depew believed that. And yet the power of her symbolism could be appropriated by populists and by progressives—politicians who stood for change and social reorganization—men like William Jennings Bryan and Theodore Roosevelt.

She would attain the status of a goddess, but one who presided over a changing and improving, not just a static, society. And that guaranteed her immortality.

Even while the work of building the statue was going on, America's essence was changing. The era of clipper ships and fur traders was disappearing under a shower of revolutionary inventions and technological improvements. In the long gestation period of the statue from 1865 to 1886, the first transatlantic cable and transcontinental railroad were completed. The telephone, typewriter, phonograph, electric lights and motors, the gasoline engine and the steam turbine, steel rails, wire, and girders, and chemical dyes made first appearances or started to come into common use. Mechanical cultivators, harvesters, and threshers began to turn farms into agricultural factories. Improved machinery speeded up the production of things in everyday use—canned goods and carpeting, newspapers and window glass, cigarettes and stoves, platters and sewing needles. In the 1850s the government issued about one thousand patents a year. By the 1870s the government was awarding that many in a single month.

After 1886 the pace increased. Before the statue celebrated its tenth birthday in 1896, the first motion pictures had been made and the first automobile had been driven on an American street. Between then and the twentieth anniversary in 1906, the X ray and radium were discovered, the Wright Brothers flew, and Marconi sent radio signals across the Atlantic.

When Bartholdi made his first trip to the United States in 1871, he had written home to say that society in America seemed to run on rails. Thirty years later that was almost a literal truth. Nearly two hundred thousand miles of track were in operation, lacing almost every village in the country into a national network. Five great trunk lines between the Mississippi Valley and the Pacific Coast rushed settlers into the Far West. In 1889 and 1890, six new states—Washington, Idaho, Montana, North and South Dakota, and Wyoming—were added to the nation at whose gateway the statue stood. Matching the westward surge of population was the growth of the cities. When the arm and torch were first shown in Philadelphia in 1876, there were some forty-six million Americans, but barely more than a dozen places in the country with populations of more than fifty thousand. In 1901, Americans numbered seventy-five million; at least one in three of them lived in some kind of city, and of those twenty-five million urbanites, eleven million—some four out of ten—were in places with populations of better than two hundred and fifty thousand. To handle the influx, cities grew upward and outward, and became more ingenious at moving people around. New York was one of the best examples of such growth. From the statue's head, sightseers in 1886 could admire the towers of the Brooklyn Bridge, opened only three years earlier. By 1906, two more bridges spanned the East River and a third was under way—and Brooklyn, once independent, had become simply a borough of the greater city. The statue's distinction as the tallest object on the New York horizon (at 305 feet) did not last long, as skyscrapers such as the Flatiron Building (1902), the forty-seven-story Singer Building (1908), and the sixty-story Woolworth Building (1913) rose into Manhattan's skies. In 1904, the year that Bartholdi died in Paris, the first station on New York's subway system—at City Hall—was opened. As did the elevated trains and streetcars that were also recent additions to the cityscape, the subways ran on electric power, although, like the statue's torch itself, sometimes feebly. The energy of a new century was pouring from the humming wheels of the dynamo.

What was to become of liberty in the age of the dynamo? Laboulaye had been at particular pains to argue that liberty in America was law-abiding and conservative. But the history of the 1880s and 1890s called that happy view into question. The successful businessmen who built the great railroads, or took control of them through bold operations in an unregulated stock market; the owners of mines and steelworks and packing houses and oil refineries; the leading manufacturers of the grand new inventions—all counted their wealth in millions, and had forged great organizations that crowded smaller, allegedly less efficient competitors off the map. At the other end of the scale were industrial workers vulnerable to wage cuts and layoffs, and farmers who mortgaged themselves to the banks for those productive new machines,

A Symbol of Progress. Liberty on the cover of the magazine *Le Mouvement Scientifique*, December 29, 1885. *Private Collection, Paris.*

and then were brutally squeezed between falling crop prices and rising rates for transportation, interest, and supplies. In times of economic downturn, the countryside filled with drifters, and city slums were rife with the misery of the jobless. Midwestern and Southern agrarians, with a little help from labor, organized a protesting third major party in 1892, the Populist or People's party. Its first national platform declared: "From the same prolific womb of…injustice, we produce the two great classes, tramps and millionaires."

When the statue was dedicated in October 1886, the talk of the whole country was of the Haymarket riot in Chicago six months earlier. At a protest meeting growing out of a strike at the McCormick Harvester works, someone had thrown a bomb, killing seven policemen. In a trial full of hysteria, eight anarchists were found guilty on flimsy evidence, and four were hanged.

The talk of New York City was of the mayoral campaign just concluding, almost literally under the statue's nose. The most controversial candidate was Henry George, who had written seven years earlier that modern progress only served "to build up great fortunes, to increase luxury and make sharper the contrast between the House of Have and the House of Want." His solution was for society to appropriate, and use for the benefit of all, the entire increase in land values that progress had made possible. Running on this single-tax platform, he came in behind Democrat Abram S. Hewitt, but ahead of the young and wealthy Republican candidate, Theodore Roosevelt.

Throughout the 1890s the tempo of social conflict increased. A bitter strike over a wage cut at the Homestead steel works in 1892 led to a pitched battle between workers and strikebreakers. Ten men died in gunfire. That year the Populists, who called, among other things, for nationalizing the railroads and telegraphs and the institution of an income tax, picked up twenty-two electoral votes. The following year a severe depression hit the economy, and in 1894 a walkout to protest wage cuts at the Pullman railroad-car factory on the outskirts of Chicago turned into a nationwide sympathy strike of railroad workers. President Cleveland called out federal troops to break the strike, but riots in various cities led to more killings. Millions of dollars' worth of boxcars and warehouses were destroyed by fire. The strike's leader, Eugene V. Debs, went to jail, from which he emerged as a Socialist; later he would run four times for President on that party's ticket. That fall the Populists won about a dozen congressional seats and a number of state and local offices. In 1896 they chose to support the Democratic nominee, William Jennings Bryan, who focused his efforts on winning the country over to the artificial inflation of currency—

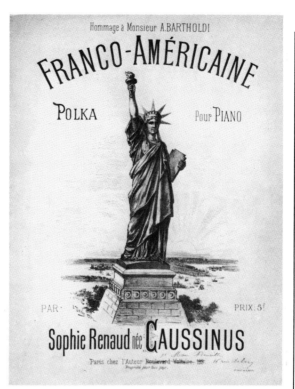

which would raise farm prices and shrink farm debts—through the unlimited coinage of silver, then in plentiful supply. He was thoroughly beaten, but only after a campaign in which the Republican supporters of William McKinley painted him as not just an ignoramus, but an anarchist and an enemy of civilization.

Hindsight would show that the country was fundamentally sound, but there was a widespread feeling that it was on the brink of civil war between forces crudely personified by men like Carnegie, Rockefeller, Morgan, and Vanderbilt on the one hand, and by Debs, George, and the Populists on the other.

The return of good times after 1897 restored some calm, and then the brief, victorious Spanish-American War of 1898 to free Cuba brought a flush of unity. However, there was a divisive aftermath. The United States took over Spain's former colonies, including the Philippine Islands, which were not disposed to be Americanized and wanted full independence. It took seventy thousand United States troops and three years of bitter jungle fighting to "convince" them otherwise. A small but vocal and well-placed minority of American anti-imperialists, from a mixture of motives, vainly denounced the war as atrocious and immoral. "Native" people, they protested, should not and could not be forced into the American framework without destroying it.

Social critics of every variety seemed to be saying that the American republic, as created in the 1790s and preserved in the Civil War, could not live with trusts, big cities, and empire.

Yet that was the republic for which the Statue of Liberty was built. Would it have any meaning for the United States of the twentieth century? Would it have a living, everyday impact? Or would it simply be a pious memorial to good intentions and a cherished but vanished way of life—like the statue of a Minute Man on some New England village green?

The odds seemed to say that the giant statue would not "live" except as a tourist attraction. It was not very much visited, commented on, or alluded to in the 1890s. Even its mammoth proportions, impressive as they were, had less of an effect on the public's imagination as each year went by and other wonders of the modern world were unveiled.

But the statue did have a powerful future ahead of it, mainly because of its location. In choosing Bedloe's Island, Bartholdi had been more prophetic than he knew. His statue would not be out of the mainstream of modern life. He had placed it at the very focal point of one of the greatest of those transforming forces that swept over the late nineteenth-century world—immigration.

A Statue of Liberty made entirely of corn, oats, and wheat represented the farmers of Nebraska at the 1885 Exposition in New Orleans. *Harper's Weekly, January 17, 1885. American Library in Paris.*

The dynamic social forces that were at work in America were shaking Europe and Asia too, jarring loose millions of people, setting off what Americans today often forget was a worldwide movement of population, from economically stagnant regions toward those caught up in the drama of modernization.

Where the railroad, the factory, and the city took root in Europe they brought growth and prosperity. But large parts of the Continent were passed over by industrialization. Many people had to struggle with overpopulation and underemployment, archaic and unproductive landowning and farming practices, and local governments too poor or too indifferent to provide helpful services as basic as public sanitation and education. In places like Ireland, southern Italy, and large parts of the Balkans, a rural family could expect little of the future except for continued poverty, illiteracy, and chronic sickness. Tiny handfuls of small businessmen, professionals, and skilled workers in country towns faced prospects that were only a little less bleak.

Within the illustration:
NO PAYMENT OF UNMATURED NATIONAL DEBTS.
FREE TRADE IN SHIPS.
LESS POLITICS AND MORE BUSINESS
A SILVER DOLLAR THE UNIT OF VALUE,
A NAVY TO PROTECT OUR COASTS.
A TARIFF THAT WILL HELP NOT HINDER.
MORE PUBLIC WORKS,
A BETTER CIVIL SERVICE.

Left:

Popular demands. A dollar based
on silver, fairer tariffs, more employment, less corruption—these are
Liberty's demands to President
Hayes. *The Daily Graphic, May 19,
1877. Bibliothèque du Conservatoire
National des Arts et Métiers, Paris.*

Liberty on guard. Liberty
watches approvingly as the *World*
assails the whiskey interests. *Harper's Weekly, September 17, 1885.
American Library in Paris.*

For the venturesome, however, emigration provided a solution, and emigration became considerably
easier after the 1880s, when competing railroad and steamship lines began to offer cut-rate fares.
Hundreds of thousands left their villages in search of opportunity. Some went only as far as nearby cities to
find jobs. A great many went to the countries of Latin America. And small groups, especially those lucky
enough to start with a little capital, skill, or education, went to Canada and Australia, or to British, French,
and German colonies in Africa and Indochina. But enormous numbers chose America. Although it had
already enticed and absorbed millions of immigrants, America had more land, more opportunities. Its
very name, the New World, struck in everyone's heart the echo of the universal yearning for a fresh
beginning. Popular literature, translated and sold abroad, peopled America with heroic loners like the
trapper and the cowboy. Popular mythology, fed by accounts of immigrant success, painted it as a place
where enterprise was immediately rewarded with showers of money.

America had all these attractions, and it had political freedom. The appeal of liberty was universal and timeless. It was especially strong, in the late nineteenth century, among the Slavic peoples buried within the sprawling old multinational empires of Austria-Hungary, Russia, and Turkey. Poles, Czechs, Serbs, Croats, Slovenes, and Macedonians all yearned for autonomy. But just when their own cultural pride was peaking, it clashed with the equally awakened nationalism of the German, Hungarian, Russian, and Ottoman dynasties that controlled the imperial governments in Vienna, St. Petersburg, and Constantinople. These "superpowers" launched campaigns to stamp out the languages, religions, traditions, and organizations of their "inferior" subject peoples. This, they argued, would modernize and unify their domains. As always, pressure fell most heavily on those quintessential outsiders, the Jews, especially in Russia where there was a long tradition of anti-Semitism. In the 1880s, by order of the Tsar, they were confined to a small and undeveloped part of Russian Poland, denied access to schooling, the professions, and land ownership, and made the targets of government-sanctioned hate campaigns and pogroms.

To them—as to everyone who had, for whatever reason, been muzzled, jailed, tormented, or even excluded—America meant something more than simply the chance to get rich. So when the urge to try their luck elsewhere came over them, they chose America.

And America was ready to be chosen. With rare exceptions, its policy had always been to keep the door open for newcomers. From colonial times this made practical economic sense in a raw land that needed settlers. The American Revolution added a moral dimension, with Thomas Paine's plea, in *Common Sense*: "Every spot of the Old World is overrun with oppression. Freedom hath been hunted round the globe.... O! receive the fugitive and prepare in time an asylum for mankind." This combination of high-minded and down-to-earth considerations remained the bedrock of the liberal immigration policy adopted by the new country.

Between 1820 and 1860 more than five million Europeans migrated to the United States. The largest single groups were more than a million and a half Irish, most of them fleeing a devastating famine in their homeland, and about an equal number of Germans. When post–Civil War expansion went into high gear in the 1880s, the numbers began to increase dramatically. In 1881 the annual "intake" went over the half-million mark for the first time to 669,431, and in 1882 it was 788,992. In that year, Congress chose to keep nonwhites out of the "asylum for mankind." It barred Chinese immigration. Three years later, responding to some pressure from the young labor movement (the precursor of the American Federation of Labor was then four years old), it passed the Foran Act. This legislation prevented the importation of cheap labor by forbidding employers to sign workers abroad to contracts for jobs in the United States. Bills were also introduced in the eighties to bar chronic invalids, mental deficients, convicts, and paupers.

Despite such restrictions, the American message was an unusual one among sovereign nations. It offered Europeans the opportunity to enter the country with virtually no requirements, restrictions, or special burdens before or after admission, and to become citizens quickly and easily. In short it said: "There is plenty to do. Come on over."

And come they did. Seven times between 1883 and 1903 the yearly total passed half a million. In 1905 for the first time it went slightly over a million, stayed there in 1906, and hit a record 1,285,349 in 1907. Three times in the next six years immigration totals exceeded a million, and in the other three were never less than three-quarters of a million. Roughly speaking, some thirteen million immigrants arrived between 1860 and 1900, and thirteen or fourteen million more between then and 1914, when World War I temporarily cut off the flow. Another four million came during the twenties. By the mid-1980s, it would be a fair guess that perhaps one American in four was descended from this mighty wave of people, thirty million strong, shifting from one side of the Atlantic to the other.

Almost all of those who came after 1900 were from southern and eastern Europe. Almost all of them landed in New York, which had become the major terminus of passenger traffic across the north Atlantic. They steamed through the Narrows between Brooklyn and Staten Island, and their first sight of America was of the broad, busy Upper Bay, the New York and New Jersey skyline, and the Statue of Liberty.

Their acquaintance with the statue turned out to be close and occasionally lengthy, because in 1892 the

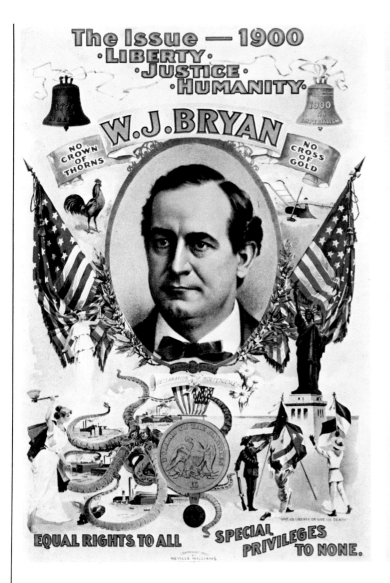

federal government opened an immigration reception station at Ellis Island, only a short distance away.

Its unprepossessing history was much like that of Bedloe's Island. Known to the Indians as Kilshk, or Gull Island, it was bought by the Dutch and used for oyster fishing. After the Revolution it came into the possession of one Samuel Ellis. The United States acquired it for a harbor fortification during the War of 1812, and both the Army and the Navy used it as a munitions depot until 1890. When federal immigration officials were first considering various locations to replace the outdated and overcrowded facility in Castle Garden at the foot of Manhattan, they gave some thought to Bedloe's Island itself. Bartholdi, on hearing of this possibility in Paris, criticized the idea as "monstrous," but he had no cause to worry, since Ellis Island was the final choice.

The first wooden building on Ellis Island in which the new arrivals were processed was destroyed by fire in 1897. A competition for a new one was won by the architectural firm of Boring and Tilton. Edward Tilton had studied, like Richard Hunt, at the Ecole des Beaux-Arts, and his victorious design called for a huge, formal hall with towers and arched windows, in the style of a great European railway station.

It was into this gigantic Beaux-Arts vault that the immigrants were shepherded. Those, that is, who could afford to pay only the cheapest fares. When the steamers docked in the city, first- and second-class passengers were questioned aboard ship by the inspectors. All the others were placed on ferries, taken back out into the bay, and deposited, bag, baggage, and children, on the wharf at Ellis Island.

Top left:

Liberty, Justice, Humanity was one of William Jennings Bryan's campaign slogans emblazoned across this poster. *Library of Congress.*

The cult of the golden calf. The goddess Liberty dethroned by King Dollar. *Puck, July 3, 1912. Library of Congress.*

Depending on circumstances, the experience of processing could be simple or harrowing. Basically it consisted of a rudimentary physical examination for contagious or crippling diseases, and an interrogation to find out if the newcomer had a criminal record or was likely to become a public charge. When traffic was light, it was quickly completed. But on the many days when as many as three thousand people or more swarmed into the reception hall, the process became arduous. Tired immigrant families waited for hours in long lines, separated by stockyardlike railings, totally bewildered by the strange surroundings and incomprehensible questions and commands, which at best were poorly and hastily translated by overworked interpreters. The clothes of anyone who seemed to require more intensive examination would be marked with colored chalk, the person set aside in a detention pen, without benefit of explanation. Some might be held on the island in a limbo of uncertainty for several days or longer. Worse than all the small and unavoidable humiliations was the fear of the final judgment—of being told, after the years of planning, saving, suffering, and the pain of leave-taking, that one was inadmissible and had to go back.

Only a relative few had to endure this heartbreak. Most went on to be greeted by waiting relatives and jobs. But the mere prospect of rejection was a shadow that overhung the stay on Ellis Island. For those few hours, the immigrants were fused into a living mass suspended between two existences. The Old World was behind them, but they were not yet in the New. Gathered from every corner of Europe and speaking in many tongues, stripped of individuality by the processing, gnawed by anxiety, they lacked any identifiable group characteristic except one.

What they had in common was expectation. They had taken the gamble of change. However poor their beginnings, they had chosen not simply to wait for what the future would bring, but to fling themselves into the future and become the architects of their own fate. America, they believed, gave them that opportunity. Freedom was not merely the chance to earn a dollar or to cast a vote. It was the chance to become something else, something better.

And America was first visible to them in the imposing, unforgettable, 305-foot-high presence of the Statue of Liberty. Many, perhaps most of them, had heard of it. But when the sight of it actually burst upon them, it spoke directly and powerfully to their feelings in a language that needed no interpreters. Edward Corsi, who in time would himself become a United States Commissioner of Immigration, saw it from the deck of the *Florida*, fourteen days out of Naples, in 1907: "Passengers all about us were crowding to the rail. Jabbered conversation, sharp cries, laughs and cheers—a steadily rising din filled the air. Mothers and fathers lifted up the babies so that they too could see, off to the left, the Statue of Liberty.... Looming shadowy through the mist, it brought silence to the decks.... This symbol of America—this enormous expression of what we had all been taught was the inner meaning of this new country we were coming to—inspired awe."

A little more earthy was the reaction of young Arnold Weiss in 1921: "Seeing the Statue of Liberty was the greatest thing I've ever seen. It was really something…. To know you're in this country. God, just think of it…. I said to myself, 'Gee, we're in America. Now I can go out in the streets and pick up gold.' "

Celia Rypinski, a Polish immigrant girl, prayed when she saw it. And Sarah Asher from Russia, another unremarkable member of the thirty million, told an interviewer of how she had gotten up at five A.M. with all her fellow passengers: "The sunshine started, and what do we see? The Statue of Liberty!…Well, she was beautiful with the early morning light. Everybody was crying. The whole boat bent toward her because everybody went out, everybody, everybody was in the same spot. We had been sinking and we survived and now we were looking at the Statue of Liberty. She was beautiful with the sunshine so bright.

The Steerage. Alfred Stieglitz's 1907 photograph is one of the best-known images of European immigration to America. *Zabriskie Gallery, Paris.*

Top:

Ellis Island. Way-station in the shadow of the Statue of Liberty for millions of future Americans. *Statue of Liberty National Monument, New York.*

Italian family at Ellis Island in 1905. Photograph by Lewis Hine. *Statue of Liberty National Monument, New York.*

Beautiful colors, the greenish-like water—and so big, and everybody was crying." The captain, alarmed by the list the ship was taking, came down to the deck and pleaded with the crowd to move back. After a while, he saw how it was with his passengers. He simply said, "All right," and gave up.

Neither Bartholdi nor Laboulaye had ever suggested associating the statue with the American promise of new life for the downtrodden of the earth. Nor had any of the speakers at the inauguration ceremonies. Cleveland, Evarts, and Depew hailed the statue as a monument to peace and international friendship, to liberty as an ideal and a historic force, and to the progress it had made and inspired in the world since American independence.

Just when these abstractions seemed to have been drained of relevance in the social tumult of the new country's expansion, the immigrant influx had moved in to fill the gap and revitalize the statue as an icon. Who could have foreseen it?

One person had, and had, moreover, expressed this particular meaning of the statue in powerful and beautiful language three years before the inauguration, though hardly anyone knew it at the time. Her name was Emma Lazarus.

She herself was not poor, she was not an immigrant, she never married, and she did not live to see Ellis Island open its doors. She was the daughter of Moses Lazarus, a rich New York sugar refiner, part of the elite community of New York's Sephardic Jews who traced their ancestry back to medieval Spain and

Immigrants being examined for **trachoma** at Ellis Island. Evidence of the eye disease meant rejection by the New World. *Public Health Service in the National Archives.*

Portugal. Her mother's kinfolk, the Nathans, were equally wealthy and distinguished, and Emma's uncles and cousins included stockbrokers, railroad directors, and a future Supreme Court Justice, Benjamin N. Cardozo.

Born in 1849, she was educated by private tutors and showed a precocious gift for poetry and languages. Her father, whom she adored, had her first volume of verses—her own and translations from French and German poets—privately printed the year she turned seventeen. She met Ralph Waldo Emerson at a party and sent him a copy. They became lifelong friends and correspondents. By the time she was thirty-one, she had published a novel and a play as well as more poems and translations. Most of her work was in a nineteenth-century romantic style that now survives only in anthologies, but her contemporary reputation was strong.

Until 1881 Emma was not an especially committed Jew. When the rabbi of Shearith Israel, her father's congregation, asked if she would help him with a new translation of a prayer book, her answer was that she would try but could not contribute much. "I shall always be loyal to my race, but I feel no religious fervor in my soul." She thought of herself as cosmopolitan, which was not surprising. Moses Lazarus and his family were freely accepted almost everywhere in New York society, and there was not an important figure in the magazine and publishing world that Emma did not know as a friend.

Then came a dramatic change. Following the assassination of Tsar Alexander II, a vicious and violent wave of anti-Semitism swept through Russia. Hundreds of thousands of refugees streamed toward safety in other countries, where they were sheltered and fed by quickly organized rescue societies. One small group wound up in temporary barracks on Ward's Island in the East River. Like most civilized Americans, both Jews and Gentiles, Emma was outraged by what she had heard. As a member of an assistance committee, she visited the island, and was transformed by what she saw. It was apparently her first good look at poor Jews, Orthodox Jews, and above all, persecuted Jews. It released a flood of emotional loyalty in her.

With great intensity she took up the cause of "her people." During 1882 she attended protest meetings and wrote brilliantly argued pieces on Jews and Judaism for important magazines. She began to learn Hebrew, showed interest in the embryonic Zionist movement, and published another volume of poems, entitled *Songs of a Semite*. But her conversion was not to a purely parochial viewpoint. Jews were not all sages and martyrs. They shared, she wrote, "the dualism of humanity; they are made up of the good and the bad." All humanity suffered when evil was done to any part of it. For one of her articles, she borrowed the words of William M. Evarts, spoken at a meeting on behalf of pogrom victims. The issue was not simply "the oppression of Jews by Russians." It was "the oppression of men and women by men and women. And *we are men and women*."

In the autumn of 1883, just after Lazarus had returned from a trip to England, Evarts came to her, not only as a friend, but as chairman of the American Committee for the Statue of Liberty, with a request. There was to be a literary auction to raise money for the pedestal. Manuscripts by Walt Whitman, Mark Twain, and Bret Harte would be on sale, and he wondered if she would contribute a poem in her own hand. She hesitated a little, claiming that she hated to write "to order." But in the last week of November she sent the committee a sonnet.

Popular descriptions of the statue had compared it time and again to the Colossus of Rhodes, something that Bartholdi himself would have approved of. Lazarus saw "The New Colossus" in an altogether different light:

Not like the brazen giant of Greek fame,
With conquering limbs astride from land to land;
Here at our sea-washed, sunset gates shall stand
A mighty woman with a torch, whose flame
Is the imprisoned lightning, and her name
Mother of Exiles. From her beacon-hand

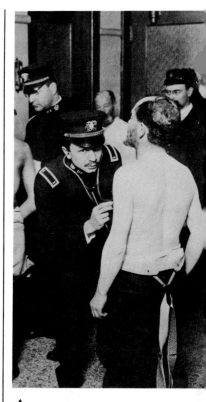

An immigrant undergoes medical examination at Ellis Island, early 1900s. *Library of Congress.*

Glows world-wide welcome; her mild eyes command
The air-bridged harbor that twin cities frame.

"Keep, ancient lands, your storied pomp!" cries she
With silent lips. "Give me your tired, your poor,
Your huddled masses yearning to breathe free,
The wretched refuse of your teeming shore.
Send these, the homeless, tempest-tost to me.
I lift my lamp beside the golden door!"

The published sonnet attracted little attention, although James Russell Lowell wrote to Lazarus to say: "I liked your sonnet about the Statue much better than I like the Statue itself.... [It] gives its subject a *raison d'être* which it wanted before quite as much as it wanted a pedestal."

It was not a view that anyone else seemed to share. Lazarus left New York in the spring of 1885, after her father's death, for an extended trip to England and Europe. There she first became aware that she had Hodgkin's disease, a form of cancer. The affliction struck her while she was still developing her poetic and polemical abilities, and cut short her life and career. She was in Paris when the statue was inaugurated. Wasted and pain-wracked, she came back to New York in July 1887, just after her thirty-eighth birthday. There is no record of what she thought when she first laid eyes on the statue itself. Less than four months later she was dead.

By 1903 history had caught up with her poem. It was one of those cases where life imitates art. The statue had become indelibly associated with the steady tide of migration flowing past it. That year a woman named Georgina Schuyler, who had been Emma Lazarus's admiring friend, arranged to have "The New Colossus" engraved on a plaque inside the pedestal. Even then, there were no speeches, no ceremonies, no press coverage. Nevertheless, the poem took hold. Reprinted, anthologized, assigned to students, the sonnet gradually became as familiar as the statue itself and has remained so. In 1949 Irving Berlin composed a musical, *Miss Liberty*, for which he set the final five lines to music, introducing them to

The New Colossus.

Not like the brazen giant of Greek fame,
With conquering limbs astride from land to land;
Here at our sea-washed, sunset-gates shall stand
A mighty woman with a torch, whose flame
Is the imprisoned lightning, and her name
Mother of Exiles. From her beacon-hand
Glows world-wide welcome; her mild eyes command
The air-bridged harbor that twin-cities frame.

"Keep, ancient lands, your storied pomp!" cries she
With silent lips. "Give me your tired, your poor,
Your huddled masses yearning to breathe free,
The wretched refuse of your teeming shore,
Send these, the homeless, tempest-tost to me,
I lift my lamp beside the golden door!"

Emma Lazarus.

November 2nd 1883.

additional millions who possibly assumed that Lazarus was present at the creation of the monument. She was not, but she belongs with Laboulaye, Bartholdi, Eiffel, and Pulitzer in the gallery of those who gave it life. (The original manuscript of the sonnet is in the Library of the American Jewish Historical Society.)

Officialdom was not quick to link the statue and the immigrant. When Woodrow Wilson dedicated an improved lighting system for the torch in 1916, his words would not have been out of place thirty years earlier. President Cleveland had then said: "We shall not forget that Liberty has here made her home, nor shall her chosen altar be neglected." Wilson appeared to add an afterthought with these words: "There is a great responsibility in having adopted Liberty as an ideal, because we must illustrate it in what we do."

But when Franklin D. Roosevelt spoke on the statue's fiftieth anniversary, in 1936, he went directly to the subject of immigration. Though he did not say so explicitly, his words of praise challenged any possible unfortunate misinterpretation of the phrase "wretched refuse." The immigrants had not been merely passive, helpless outcasts. In reality, they were: "men and women who had the supreme courage to strike out for themselves, to abandon language and relatives, to start at the bottom without influence, without money, and without knowledge of a life in a very young civilization. We can say for all America what the Californians say of the Forty-niners: 'The cowards never started and the weak died by the way.' "

But there was irony in the tribute. For by then, the golden door had been closed for more than ten years.

The steady influx of immigrants was indispensable in furnishing the labor that built industrial America, but it generated its own backlash. There had been rumblings of nativism in the 1850s, mainly directed at the Irish, who were Catholic and poor. These rumblings had subsided at the time of the Civil War, but were now reawakened in the ferment of the 1890s. The mere numbers of the immigrants gave some Americans whose roots ran back three, four, or more generations a disturbing sense that they were becoming a minority. And the shift in the ethnic composition of the annual arrivals at Ellis Island was equally disturbing, especially to those who took inordinate pride in their English descent, a group that included a good share of the country's cultural leaders. For them, "Anglo-Saxon institutions" and "American institutions" were identical terms, and they saw both being threatened by a "new" immigration that was heavily Italian, Jewish, and Slavic, and that they wanted very badly to restrict.

The restrictionists argued that the "old" immigrants from Germany, Scandinavia, and the British Isles

great melting pot, it should not pour its contents into exclusively Anglo-Saxon molds. The restrictionists were joined by organized labor, whose viewpoint was expressed by the AFL's perennial president, Samuel Gompers (himself a Dutch-born Jewish immigrant): "Cheap labor, ignorant labor, takes our jobs and cuts our wages." The political weight of the restriction movement steadily increased. Congress kept adding to the list of aliens who might be excluded on moral or medical grounds—paupers, prostitutes, polygamists, epileptics, anarchists, and sufferers from "loathsome" (i.e., venereal) diseases. Three times between 1896 and 1915 it passed bills requiring a literacy test for immigrants, but three separate Presidents vetoed the measures.

World War I and its immediate aftermath gave the restrictionists another chance. Fears of Bolsheviks and German spies merged with a general, frantic drive for conformity that crushed the opposition to tight control of immigration. It was impossible to make headway against arguments like that of the Tennessee legislator who declared: "We get the majority of the communists.... the dynamiters, and the assassins of public officers from the ranks of the present-day immigrant."

In 1921 and 1922 Congress passed temporary measures setting up a national-origins quota system. This limited the admissible yearly number of immigrants of each nationality to the percentage of people of that nationality in the population as of 1910. The purpose was to provide the smallest quotas for the groups that had come most recently. The Johnson-Reed Act of 1924 made these restrictions permanent.

Right:

"**Y**ou buy a Liberty Bond." Poster from the first Liberty Loan drive in 1917, with Liberty taking Uncle Sam's traditional pose. *Statue of Liberty National Monument, New York.*

Far right:

That Liberty Shall Not Perish. The fourth Liberty Loan campaign placed Liberty in a fiery sky and echoed a resounding phrase from Lincoln's Gettysburg address. *Statue of Liberty National Monument, New York.*

Bottom left:

The Safest Investment in the World. By 1919, Liberty was wearing a modern gown of stars and stripes and advertising Victory Bonds. *Statue of Liberty National Monument, New York.*

Bottom right:

Food Will Win the War. Designed and written to appeal to recent immigrants, this poster was translated into all the languages spoken in the United States. *Statue of Liberty National Monument, New York.*

When stripped of various exceptions, timetables, and special provisions, it said that no more than 150,000 immigrants from outside the Western Hemisphere could be allowed entry into the country in any year. When the first of these provisions went into effect, it became clear how thoroughly the new legislation discriminated against southern and eastern Europeans. More than half of all 150,000 spaces were reserved for residents of the British Isles, whereas only 5,802 Italians and 6,524 Poles could be admitted. Asians continued to be barred altogether.

By this stroke, the statue was basically deprived of its meaning as a symbol of America's welcome to all, even though the image lingered long after the reality had changed. The Johnson-Reed Act remained in force for more than forty years. It did not prevent a small but distinguished migration of refugee intellectuals in the 1930s, and it was modified piecemeal after World War II, to accommodate still other waves of refugees. But attempts at a complete, liberalizing overhaul of immigration policy were beaten back. One such defeat came in 1952, when the McCarran-Walter Act was passed. Ostensibly it provided for changes, but in fact it was more restrictive than its predecessors. Senator John F. Kennedy, an opponent, sardonically argued that Emma Lazarus's poem should be rewritten to say: "Give me your tired, your poor…as long as they come from northern Europe, are not too tired or too poor or slightly ill, never stole a loaf of bread, never joined any questionable organization, and can document their activities for the past two years."

It was not until 1965 that a totally new immigration law was enacted. It scrapped the national-origins quotas, but it was not a return to the wide-open past. An overall annual ceiling of 170,000 Western Hemisphere immigrants was retained, and a temporary limit of 120,000 within the hemisphere was imposed. There was also a new quota system, based on skills and on kinship with American citizens.

President Johnson signed the measure in a ceremony at the base of the Statue of Liberty. By this time the gesture was purely sentimental. Immigrants now came by air. And Ellis Island, closed and neglected since 1954, was falling into ruins. Yet the President knew that the statue was still a powerful presence in the national imagination. Liberty's day of lifting the lamp beside the golden door was long gone, but the statue had survived in another symbolic role, that of America itself, and become stronger than ever with the passage of time.

Paradoxically, it was World War I, which had accelerated the end of unlimited immigration and of the statue's death as "mother of exiles," that was also responsible for still another symbolic rebirth.

On April 6, 1917, the United States entered World War I on the side of the Allies, after two years and eight months of gradually dwindling neutrality. A major cause of war was the German submarine campaign against neutral shipping, but freedom of the seas, as an issue, was quickly buried under an avalanche of more far-reaching propaganda. America embraced the contention of France and Great Britain that they were not self-interested nations defending their power and influence in the world, but free peoples protecting themselves against the assault of German autocracy and militarism. President Wilson, strongly endowed with a missionary's temperament, carried the line farther. The goal of victory, he proclaimed, should not just be the defeat of Germany, but of arbitrary power everywhere. He announced a glittering fourteen-point peace program. Independent nationhood for all European peoples. An end to arms races and tariff wars. No more secret treaties. An impartial adjustment of colonial claims (apparently colonies would always exist)—and a League of Nations. Altogether these would bring about the abolition of armed conflict, and release the energies of freedom to triumph everywhere. America, his rhetoric announced, was not merely in a new war, but a final conflict—a war to end wars. America was not part of an ongoing power struggle. It was engaged in a crusade to make the world safe for democracy.

But democracy was a word that merely suggested a form of government. Its appeal as a rallying cry was limited. There were deeper, louder, and farther-reaching echoes in the word "liberty."

A gigantic modern public relations apparatus began to mobilize the home front for sacrifices on behalf of liberty. That campaign required a unifying symbol, and there was none better than the statue itself. Early in the war, embattled America was represented on posters as Uncle Sam, squinting and pointing his finger at military-age males with the command: "I Want You." But the appeal of Uncle Sam was limited. He represented the part of the national character that was folksy, practical, and down-to-earth. It was hard to think of him in connection with highflown terms like nobility and sacrifice. Besides Uncle Sam there was also the nineteenth-century female figure of Columbia. But she was already a little dated, a little too romantic and abstract. She bore the same relation to the Statue of Liberty that some of the lofty and static "official" poetry written for the inauguration bore to Lazarus's poem, with its vibrant and direct imagery.

Columbia was still only an imaginary figure. But the Statue of Liberty actually existed. It was there, palpable, three decades old, rising with impressive solidity from the middle of the port of New York. Columbia was distant, illusory. Liberty had already become the mother of exiles. As a more mundane consideration, Liberty had been appearing in advertisements for years, and had shown an uncanny power to enhance any sales message. In so doing, the statue had become even more of a familiar presence.

So it was Liberty who appeared on billboards everywhere, urging Americans on to the collective civilian efforts that a modern war required. The statue "worked" for the War Food Administration, urging housewives to conserve food for export by saving fats, growing home gardens, and observing wheatless and meatless days. Above all, it was vital to the Department of the Treasury in floating five popular loan drives that raised approximately fifteen billion dollars toward defraying the costs of the war.

These campaigns were something special. Governments had always raised taxes and borrowed money to fight wars, but usually from wealthy banks. The "Liberty Loans" of 1917 and 1918 were different. They were designed to involve ordinary people, who could buy "Liberty Bonds" in denominations as small as fifty dollars or War Savings Certificates, that could be traded in later for bonds, for as little as five dollars. There were even twenty-five-cent War Savings Stamps for schoolchildren. Every purchaser became an investor in the war, so that the loans were instruments both of fund raising and of total mobilization.

Various Liberty Bond posters were targeted to particular audiences, and among these were the millions of recent immigrants. One of them showed an incoming vessel, along whose deck railings the newcomers were lined up as she approached the statue. "Remember Your First Thrill of American Liberty," it trumpeted. The implication was obvious: gratitude required support of the war.

In this way the war contributed to the assimilation of the immigrants even while the restriction movement was poised for final victory. Both the unifying and the repressive effects of the patriotic fever were felt. Those aliens who had any connection with either the German enemy or radical movements were vigorously denounced and harassed; German-Americans, in spite of being part of the admired "old" immigration, had a particularly hard time. But those who willingly abandoned their "foreign" outlooks, who paid the price of admission by contributing their sons and their dollars to America's crusade, were made to feel part of the national family.

Identifying Liberty with victory did not at first diminish the universality of the image. So long as people in all the Allied countries believed the Wilsonian promise that the end of the fighting would bring an era of peace and justice for humanity everywhere, the statue still belonged to the world that it was enlightening, just as Bartholdi had always believed it should.

But in 1919 those hopes failed. A conventional victors' peace was imposed at Versailles. All Wilson could salvage of his program was the League of Nations, and the United States Senate denied him even that when it refused to allow American participation in the organization. Wilson left office a broken man, and the country withdrew into conservatism and isolation.

The 1920s left the statue shorn of some of its international character. It had become Americanized, a sign of home to thousands of cheering troops returning to New York from France's battlefields, a cartoonist's cliché for the United States. Its global reputation would thereafter be tied to the rise and fall of America's fortunes and reputation.

Yet that reputation was still magnetic, and Bartholdi's creation, at age forty, still had exactly what a monument needed, namely, a capacity to evoke passionate, widespread responses. Whatever messages it radiated—Franco-American friendship, welcome to the wanderer, embattled freedom, America the beautiful—they struck deep, and would keep on doing so.

Remember Your First Thrill of
AMERICAN LIBERTY

YOUR DUTY-*Buy*
United States Government *Bonds*
2nd Liberty Loan of 1917

CHAPTER FIVE

FROM MEMORIAL TO SHRINE

On April 22, 1886, the last stone of the Statue of Liberty's pedestal was ready to be set. When the mortar for sealing it was mixed and ready, the workers on the job pulled coins from their pockets and tossed them into the wet, gray mass. It was their modest way of making a personal contribution to the finished work.

A few months later, a young molder employed by the Hecla Company, specialists in iron construction, had almost completed his job of supervising the casting of the steps for Liberty's interior staircase. He went to his employers and asked if he might cast his initials in the last one, as a souvenir of his participation in the great project. They turned him down. Fifty years later, in 1936, he told a newspaper interviewer doing an anniversary story that he still felt the disappointment.

The same reporter unearthed another old man who had worked for the Pedestal Committee processing orders for miniatures of the statue that sold for one, two, and five dollars. Toward the end, when the subscription bandwagon was finally rolling, he had sometimes worked from 8 A.M. until 3 A.M. the next day. But his recollection was: "I felt repaid for every minute of that time."

From the very beginning, the Statue of Liberty exerted its extraordinary pull on the emotions of ordinary people.

There are two aspects to the history of a monument. One is the development of the idea that it embodies, and to which it gives an image. If that image starts to play a starring role in a people's mythology, and grows into a familiar and beloved presence, then the monument is a success. Judged by that standard, the Statue of Liberty is an absolute triumph. From the day that Pulitzer rallied his readers to pour a flood of pennies and nickels into the pedestal fund, it proved its capacity to excite the popular imagination, and that power has steadily increased through the years. It is hard to think of any comparable attraction—Plymouth Rock, the Washington Monument, the Lincoln Memorial, the Tomb of the Unknown Soldier—that exerts an appeal anywhere near as magnetic.

But there is also the story of how the nation takes care of the monument as a tangible physical reality, a structure subject to the ravages of age and overuse. This part of the statue's history is more checkered. For when the federal government took custody in 1886, it embarked on a job for which it had neither the machinery nor the experience, and which it badly fumbled. Only when the United States became more adept at managing the conservation of its historic and national resources, something which it was too much in a hurry to care about in the nineteenth century, did it start to atone for early neglect of France's gift. And only after the statue reached its seventieth birthday did the government complete the development of a fully orchestrated "official" setting for it.

On an autumn day in 1894, a city editor of the New York *Herald* dispatched a reporter to Bedloe's Island to see how the eight-year-old Statue of Liberty was faring. The first sight that greeted the *Herald*'s man as he debarked from the ferry was a U.S. artilleryman standing stiffly on sentry duty. But other, unoccupied soldiers, legs dangling, were fishing off the wharf. From it, a boardwalk led to the walls of Fort Wood. On

In 1909 the Wright Brothers made a breathtaking flight over Bedloe's Island and past the Statue of Liberty. *Harper's Weekly, October 9, 1909.*

Gutzon Borglum, a second-generation Danish sculptor, renovated and redesigned the statue's torch in 1916. Borglum, whose penchant for the gigantic culminated in Mount Rushmore, did make the torch easier to see, but his new design allowed corrosion that would damage it beyond repair. *Library of Congress.*

either side were shanties that housed a photographer's shop, a peanut and fruit stand, and a bar and restaurant whose signs promised visitors "Ice Cold Beer" and "Fresh Clam Chowder."

On the parade ground, where the seating platform used during the inauguration had not yet been taken down, a tethered Army mule named Tommy contentedly munched grass. His martial function was to haul ashes and supplies. Entering the pedestal, the correspondent saw two tablets, one proclaiming the statue to be a gift from the French to the American people, and the other declaring that the pedestal had been built by voluntary contributions. Both had been covered with plate glass, and visitors with diamond rings and a yen for immortality had scratched their names on the smooth surfaces.

The stones of the pedestal itself were too rough-textured to take writing, but there were hundreds of autographs scrawled on the masonry "pointing" between them. A lone security guard was unable to deal with hordes of graffiti-scrawlers. He was not an Army man, but a civilian hired by a citizens' committee that operated the ferry and was responsible for the care and guidance of visitors. The Army was interested only in protecting the fort and other military properties. And the Lighthouse Board, the technical custodian of the statue, was concerned only with the maintenance of the feeble torch. Under this three-headed administration, the statue was left largely unattended.

Opposite right:

A deadly flame: A few months after the dedication ceremonies, thousands of migrating birds lay stunned and dying on Liberty's observation platform, fatally attracted by the light from the flame. One morning, 13,450 birds were collected, representing more than a hundred species. *L'Illustration, October 6, 1887. Bibliothèque Forney, Paris.*

The Statue of Liberty at night, her new torch blazing welcome. *Culver Pictures, New York.*

Yet the first waves of tourists were already rolling in. A Visitors Book showed that since the first of September in 1890, approximately sixty-six thousand people had already come to look at Liberty as Bartholdi had conceived her. On a single August day in 1894, sixty-nine sightseers had troubled to sign the register. They came from eleven states and eight foreign countries.

The story that finally appeared in the *Herald*, under the heading "Liberty Disfigured," reproached the authorities for allowing "a great international monument" entrusted to their care to be daily "defaced and sacrificed by the scrawling of names and the indiscriminate dropping of peanut shells, tobacco quids, and the refuse of ham sandwich luncheons."

Yet the picniclike disorder of the scene on Bedloe's Island might also have been taken as a sign of how Americans were adopting the colossus and making themselves democratically at home in her front yard. From the earliest years they behaved as if she and they belonged to each other. In 1901 an immigrant New York businessman named William Flattau furnished striking evidence of that bond. He commissioned an ironmaker to build a fifty-five-foot-high replica of the statue and had it hoisted to the roof of his Liberty Moving and Storage Company at 43 West 64th Street, obviously to serve as an advertisement. But contemporaries of Flattau later testified that his gesture was also one of profound admiration and respect. He had a staircase installed, and a lookout hole in the back of the neck, which was later closed to shut out roosting pigeons. His one-third-sized copy of the great work is still there. In 1960 an attendant at a parking lot across the street told a reporter doing a "color" story on the Lincoln Center neighborhood: "I consider it a privilege to work under it."

The first shakeup in the statue's management came in 1902. Even the post commander at Fort Wood was outraged at the Lighthouse Board's indifference as a caretaker, and he complained to Washington that the statue's condition was now "a distinct disgrace to our country." President Theodore Roosevelt therefore administered the coup de grace to the idea that Liberty would ever become a beacon, and turned the statue over completely to the War Department. Roosevelt was himself a staunch preservationist and conservationist, and it was during his second administration, in 1906, that Congress passed an act authorizing Presidents to designate particular localities on federally owned land as national monuments, earmarked for special care by the Department of the Interior. The law was part of the Progressive movement's concern for administering the national domain efficiently, and it was the beginning of a series of moves that would finally give coherence to the management of the statue, though they unfolded at a leisurely pace. The National Park Service, the statue's present caretaker, was not created until 1916; the statue as not officially classified a monument until 1924; and the Park Service did not take charge of it until 1933.

Meanwhile, the War Department installed the first elevator in the pedestal in 1907–8. The shaft was already there, having been included in the original plans of Hunt and Stone; typically, it took two decades before money could be found to complete the project.

The year 1916 was a double milestone in the statue's life. It survived a disaster and underwent its first major overhaul. The catastrophe was a huge explosion and fire, set off by German saboteurs, in a munitions depot on a part of Jersey City known as Black Tom Island. Bedloe's Island was less than half a mile away from the island and from Jersey docks crowded with ships full of materiel for shipment to the European fronts of World War I.[1] For eight hours New York Harbor looked as if it were under bombardment. Smoke filled the skies, and the concussions broke windows throughout downtown Manhattan. But even though shells actually fell on Bedloe's Island and severely damaged several Army buildings, the statue stood serenely amidst the terrific shock waves, unshaken and unharmed except for a few bent struts and braces. Eighty-four-year-old Gustave Eiffel, still alive in France, had reason to be proud of his creation. (Bartholdi, however, had been dead since 1904, of tuberculosis. President Roosevelt had sent Mme. Bartholdi a message of condolence "in the name of the American people.")

In 1917 the torch was closed to the public, originating a rumor that the Black Tom blasts had weakened the arm. The truth was, however, that the platform around the torch, reached by a single fifty-four-rung ladder, could only accommodate twelve adventurous tourists at a time, and congestion had become an

Opposite:

Liberty for All. Lace crocheted by Mrs. Theodore Pilcher. *Statue of Liberty National Monument, New York.*

The great American symbols. Printed handkerchief made about 1947. *Cooper-Hewitt Museum, The Smithsonian Institution's National Museum of Design, New York.*

Weathervane. Made in the late nineteenth century by the J. L. Mott Ironworks, New York. *Collection of Ralph O. Esmerian, New York.*

Top right:

Pocket watch. Made of gold, rubies, sapphires, and a diamond, sometime after 1909. The scene represents the Wright brothers' flight over the Statue of Liberty on October 9, 1909. *Collection of Ralph O. Esmerian, New York.*

Opposite, top left:

Mantel clock with an etched glass representation of Liberty, made by E. Ingraham and Company about 1885. *Statue of Liberty National Monument, New York.*

Opposite, top right:

Plate celebrating the Fête des Ecoles in Neuilly-sur-Seine, France, 1885. *Bartholdi Museum, Colmar.*

Bottom left:

Lamp with a clock incorporated into the base, made during the late nineteenth century. *Statue of Liberty National Monument, New York.*

Bottom right:

Postcard published in the early twentieth century by the Illinois Postcard Company in New York. *Statue of Liberty National Monument, New York.*

Opposite, center left:

Calendar for the year 1887. The statue had just been inaugurated. *Private Collection, Paris.*

Opposite, bottom right:

Stained-glass window. Ordered by Joseph Pulitzer of the New York *World* in 1890, the window was originally installed in the newspaper offices. It is now located at the Columbia School of Journalism in New York. *Graduate School of Journalism, Columbia University, New York.*

Opposite, bottom left:

Cookie tin made about 1910. *Statue of Liberty National Monument, New York.*

STATUE OF LIBERTY, N.Y. CITY.

Bartholdi notre ancien Président, ses amis de la Marmite, Avril 1887.

insoluble problem. Reporters, photographers, and others with special permission could continue to make the climb and gaze down 305 feet to the water from the torch, which swayed visibly in a good breeze. It was, as one of them reported, not an experience for anyone with a fear of heights.

The renovation of 1916 involved the star-crossed lighting system. In 1892 the portholes cut in the torch flame had been replaced by a solid band of glass eighteen inches high and a skylight, but the change brought no noteworthy improvement in luminosity. As her thirtieth birthday approached, Liberty continued to enlighten the world metaphorically, while on an earthly plane she was virtually invisible after

Opposite:

A worker on Liberty's head repairs the crown. The Department of the Interior, through its Parks Service, restored Liberty's headdress in time for the opening of the New York World's Fair in July 1938. *UPI/ Bettmann Newsphotos, New York.*

A workman overhauls a spike from the statue's crown during the 1938 renovation. *UPI/Bettmann Newsphotos, New York.*

dusk. Ralph Pulitzer, who had taken over the editorship of the *World* from his father, who died in 1911, led a fresh subscription campaign among readers that raised thirty thousand dollars to correct the situation.

The work was entrusted to the sculptor Gutzon Borglum. In one sense, the choice was ideal. The American-born son of a Danish doctor and rancher from Ohio, Borglum had studied both in the United States and in Paris, and had won a reputation for doing large-scale outdoor figures. He was an ebullient patriot, a highly opinionated but not avant-garde artist, and a Westerner with a relish for the outsized. In time he would create the gigantic Mount Rushmore memorial in South Dakota—the heads of Presidents Washington, Jefferson, Lincoln, and Theodore Roosevelt, blasted out of the side of a mountain. He was as near to a twentieth-century Bartholdi as anyone could be.

But whether the original Bartholdi would have been happy with the 1916 treatment of his torch is questionable. Borglum cut six hundred small squares of copper from the flame and replaced them with amber-tinted glass, conveying, in the words of a magazine writer many years later, "the look of an outsized Tiffany lamp." With fifteen 500-candlepower gas-filled lamps inside, the torch was, in fact, easier to see, but the joints between the glass and the remaining strips of copper were not properly sealed, and Liberty's uplifted beacon leaked like a colander. Over the years, the resulting corrosion would damage the inside of the torch beyond repair.

Nevertheless, the flame "burned" brighter, and the statue was, for the first time, provided with exterior lighting from 246 projectors, each with a 250-watt floodlamp, placed strategically on the walls of the fort and on the roofs of nearby buildings.

The system was inaugurated on December 2, 1916, in one of those galas that stud the statue's history, replete with dignitaries and combining patriotism, public relations, and occasional technological razzle-dazzle. From aboard the presidential yacht *Mayflower*, Woodrow Wilson pressed a wireless key that sent an electrical impulse which turned on the new lights. He was, by right of office, the featured speaker of the occasion. But Ralph Pulitzer was there to share in the hour, and so was French Ambassador Jules Jusserand. So, too, was Chauncey M. Depew, who had delivered the "commemorative discourse" at the inauguration in 1886 and, at eighty-two, was still in pristine oratorical form. The wonderful thing about all the official speeches delivered at or near the foot of the statue was how much they resembled each other and how promptly they were forgotten.

When the speeches were completed, an aircraft piloted by "aviatrix" Ruth Law circled the statue, towing a banner with the word "Liberty." The Wright brothers had made a celebrated flight over Bedloe's Island in 1909, and there had been other planes and pilots since then, but this was the first ceremony honoring the great, female figure in which a woman played a principal part.

Four months later, France and America were once more partners in arms. But the statue remained lit throughout the wartime nights, while a Signal Corps wireless station attached to Fort Wood below squeaked out Army messages. In 1919, now weathered to its familiar light green, the statue became a cheering sight to thousands of returning troops. In the twenties, it still rode high in popular favor but sank into a fresh period of official neglect.

No important maintenance or improvement work had been undertaken since 1916, but in 1931, new improvements in the lighting system were begun. Clusters of eight 1,000-watt lights were placed at each point of the star formed by the walls of Fort Wood, and another thirteen superbright floodlights were set around the rim of the torch. This time there was no presidential kickoff to the system, but the occasion was not without theater. The 101-story Empire State Building, then the tallest skyscraper in the world, had just been completed. Mlle. Josie Laval, daughter of Premier Pierre Laval of France, was brought to the top floor, from which point she sent a radio signal to a plane flying over the statue. The signal was relayed to an electric eye that in turn set the new lights ablaze. The operation smacked somewhat of the demented inventions of cartoonist Rube Goldberg, in which hypercomplicated arrangements of objects, animals, and people performed simple tasks; but New York City's publicists were delighted with the news stories it generated, since the illuminated statue, like the Empire State Building, was now a distinctive feature of the metropolitan scene.

Subsequent lighting changes, in 1940 and 1976, have steadily enhanced Liberty's after-hours brilliance. The secret is in powerful bulbs filled with gases that modify the colors of light. Mercury and sodium vapor lamps in and around the torch gave it a more flamelike quality. Other special lights in the crown shone from the windows as if Liberty's headdress were diamond-studded. Still others, aimed upward from the pedestal, fade out the green so that under night skies her robes appear to be white.

A new elevator was installed in the pedestal. Other than that, no interior renovations were made. The result was that while Liberty looked splendid from the outside, thanks to the cosmetic effect of the new lights, the statue was suffering from serious internal problems. Most of these were the result of the constant dampness in the air rusting parts of the statue's iron framework. The air in the unheated interior of both statue and pedestal never dried out. Moreover, there was constant water seepage through popped or accidentally unclosed rivet holes at the joints of the copper plates. During the winter months, as one member of the custodial staff told a visitor, it was a good place to get rheumatism. In addition, the wear and tear of more than forty years was showing, along with a heavy accumulation of grime and graffiti.

Above:

Tourists beam down from inside the statue's head, 168 grueling steps up. Only a hardy few venture the additional 42 feet up the spiral staircase to the torch in the statue's right hand. *UPI/Bettmann Newsphotos, New York.*

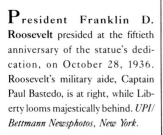

Oh, **Lady! Lady!** Cartoon by Rollin Kirby, from *The World*, December 2, 1918. *Museum of the City of New York*.

President Franklin D. **Roosevelt** presided at the fiftieth anniversary of the statue's dedication, on October 28, 1936. Roosevelt's military aide, Captain Paul Bastedo, is at right, while Liberty looms majestically behind. *UPI/ Bettmann Newsphotos, New York*.

Top left:

The Fife and Drum Corps of the Old Guard, Third U.S. Infantry from Fort Meyer, Virginia, stand at attention during cornerstone ceremonies for the new Museum of Immigration, opened at the statue's base on October 28, 1962. The Old Guard Company formed the first unit of the American Army and comprised troops who had served in George Washington's Continental Army during the Revolutionary War. *UPI/Bettmann Newsphotos, New York.*

Two Greek displaced persons kiss the ground at the Statue of Liberty's foot a day after their arrival in the United States in 1951. With thirty other Greek refugees, they had asked to come ashore first on Bedloe's Island. *Culver Pictures, New York.*

A change for the better was in the offing, however. In 1933 the National Park Service formally took charge of the two acres at the south end of Bedloe's Island on which the actual monument stands. The statue finally had a guardian agency whose exclusive responsibility was to take good care of it. Plans were drawn up for the later transfer of the remaining ten acres of the island to the Park Service, following the eventual complete departure of the Army and the razing of its remaining buildings.

Before that took place, however, there was a fiftieth-birthday gala in October 1936. Once again, the President of the United States—another Roosevelt—was present, along with the ambassador of France, who, with spectacular appropriateness to the occasion, happened to be M. André de Laboulaye, grandson of the statue's founder. Among the other participating dignitaries were the mayors of Colmar and of New York. The latter, Fiorello LaGuardia, had worked for a time as an interpreter at nearby Ellis Island.

There was no great parade for the anniversary, but a naval escort accompanied the ferry that took the official party out to Bedloe's. On board, the ocean-loving Roosevelt delighted its skipper by asking knowledgeable questions about the tricky tides in the harbor. He explained his interest, saying, "I'm a bit of a pilot myself."

At the statue the audience of more than three thousand heard, through loudspeakers, a transatlantic radio address from the President of the French Republic, René Lebrun. It was a feature that would have delighted the progressive-minded original sponsors of the statue, but Ambassador de Laboulaye, in his speech, pointed out that marvelous as change and growth might be, Liberty herself was eternal. The great sculpture, he said, was "a symbol that braves the storms of time" and "would stand unshaken in the midst of the winds that roar about its head and the waves that shatter at its feet."

Roosevelt himself spoke with an eye on the ominous situation in Europe, where Hitler and Mussolini were gathering strength and openly proclaiming the imminent doom of democracy. "Liberty and peace," he reminded listeners, "are living things. In each generation—if they are to be maintained—they must be guarded anew."

At that moment, Roosevelt and the New Deal were at the height of their popularity, just three weeks short of his landslide reelection. In the spring of 1937, the New Deal came to the statue's rescue. The National Park Service was able to call for help on the WPA, the Works Progress Administration, a vast organization set up two years earlier to put unemployed men and women to work on projects of public usefulness. For twenty months the island was closed to visitors while WPA workers scrubbed away at walls and floors, strengthened stairways and platforms, and rebuilt several of the corroded spikes of the crown on new iron frames. They began the installation of the long-desired heating system and got as far as installing radiators, but there they were stopped. In 1939 a conservative reaction had set in. Congress restructured and limited the WPA, transferred many of its functions to other agencies, and made deep cuts in its budget. Heavy federal outlays began to flow instead into a buildup of American defenses as war broke out again in Europe. The New Deal's refurbishing of the statue, like its remaking of American society, was interrupted by gunfire.

During 1937 the National Park Service took complete control of Bedloe's Island and the Army began its move out, which was nearly completed just two weeks after Pearl Harbor. For almost all of the next four years the Statue of Liberty was not illuminated at night, with one triumphant exception—D-Day, June 6, 1944.

Once more, thousands of young men on the way to European battlefields watched the shadowy figure slip by in the predawn hours during which convoys often weighed anchor. Robert E. Sherwood, a Pulitzer Prize–winning playwright, was aboard one of those troopships as a correspondent. He was so moved by the statue and the soldiers' reaction to her, that he conceived the idea of somehow getting her on the stage when the war was over. That moment became the germ of his musical comedy *Miss Liberty*.

Miss Liberty did not appear on Broadway until 1949, and when it did, it was not only a tribute to the statue, but had the earmarks of a public relations undertaking on her behalf. Sherwood had gotten the incomparable Irving Berlin to write the music. Fittingly, Berlin was both an immigrant and a World War I veteran of the Seventy-seventh Division, which had adopted the statue for its shoulder patch.

Opposite:

A replica of the statue. Crowds throng Times Square to celebrate Germany's surrender, May 7, 1945. *Wide World Photos.*

Once darkened as a wartime precaution, Liberty's torch again shines over New York Harbor on June 6, 1944, in honor of D day. *Culver Pictures.*

The collaboration failed to live up to its potential. Critics found the book—about an enterprising reporter who brings the supposed model for the statue to the United States, with the usual romantic complications—mediocre, and most of the songs were not among Berlin's most memorable.

The statue needed little in the way of publicity in the period from 1948 to 1952, however. It was frequently in the news as fresh boatloads of exiles anchored in the bay. Uprooted by fascism, communism, and war, they carried new labels—refugees, displaced persons, or simply DPs—but their burdens and hopes were identical to those of the turn-of-the-century immigrants. So was their immediate attachment to the statue. One group of thirty-two DPs on an incoming Greek vessel specifically sought and received permission to be put ashore first on Bedloe's Island.

The million and a half European immigrants admitted between 1946 and 1957 were the end of a procession, the last of the seaborne wave of new arrivals. After that, intercontinental aircraft would sweep the passenger liners from the north Atlantic. Ellis Island was closed for good in 1954. Newcomers would no longer recall the statue as their first authentically American sight, though by then its international reputation as the embodiment of American welcome was so secure that it did not matter.

Meanwhile, in 1948, the renewal of immigration focused attention on the statue's condition and needs. Unsightly piles of rubble remained from the WPA's cleanup of twelve years earlier. The wharf was in an advanced state of decay. The Army was completely gone, but two of its old and unused buildings, surrounded by weeds, were slowly moldering in full view of the visitors who now were numbered in thousands during peak vacation seasons. Spurred by public outcry, Congress appropriated approximately $110,000 for tidying up. A new pier was built, as well as a new seawall surrounding the island. The

abandoned Army structures were torn down, and a program of tree-planting, pathway paving, and other landscaping was begun.

The completion of this work in the early 1950s marked a turning point in the history of the statue. From then onward, its development as a neat, officially preserved historic site proceeded at a steady pace. Simultaneously, its image became commonplace through television and other mass media, which now had a worldwide reach. As that happened, more and more groups with a message tried to appropriate its familiarity and symbolic value for themselves. These two developments must be followed on separate tracks.

It seemed almost fated that the statue should be enlisted in the propaganda battles of the Cold War. On November 19, 1956, soon after Soviet tanks had crushed a Hungarian nationalist uprising in Budapest, a young refugee unobtrusively joined the crowd of sightseers on the first morning boat to the island. Once inside the statue he slipped away, broke a lock on the door leading to the arm, and climbed to the torch. Opening a bundle, he quickly tied three banners to the platform railing. One was a U. S. flag; a second, the flag of Hungary with a black diagonal mourning stripe; the third, a white sheet on which he had lettered: STOP THE GENOCIDE. SAVE HUNGARY.

Police quickly removed both the banners and the protester. But some time afterward, an organization known as the Crusade for Freedom got official permission to launch a flight of balloons from the statue to call attention to the plight of the captive nations.

The Soviet-American confrontation was also responsible for a major change, the renaming of Bedloe's Island. American Cold War propaganda painted the United States as the chief defender of freedom, under

Today the statue stands amid a well-paved and landscaped Liberty Island. Gianfranco Gorgoni, Woodfin Camp & Associates.

Miss Liberty on Broadway. Finale of the musical comedy by Irving Berlin that opened in New York in 1949. The book was by Robert Sherwood, the choreography by Jerome Robbins. *Billy Rose Theater Collection. The New York Public Library at Lincoln Center, Astor, Lenox and Tilden Foundations.*

attack from communism all around the world, and it was partly under the spell of this concept that Congress, in 1956, cut a link to the past by voting that henceforward, the statue would stand on Liberty Island. Bedloe's was the old-shoe kind of name by which a piece of harbor real estate picked up from one of its several owners might be known. The island's new name, Liberty, though certainly appropriate because of the statue's presence, had something of a Madison Avenue ring to it.

In later year, groups of Poles and anti-Castro Cubans made efforts to demonstrate in the shadow of the statue. On a December Sunday in 1971, a group of fifteen members of Vietnam Veterans Against the War hid themselves until after closing time and emerged from their hiding places to put barricades in front of the entrances and proclaim an "occupation." Their objective was to publicize their demands for an immediate and total United States exit from Vietnam. At the time, President Richard M. Nixon had cooled off the antiwar movement by commencing the gradual withdrawal of American ground troops. The veterans were trying to refocus attention on the fighting in Vietnam, and they chose their objective shrewdly, both in terms of impact and identification. As they were removed, after a forty-eight-hour peaceable standoff, one said to a reporter: "We got the war back on Page One, where it belongs." The leader of the demonstration added: "The reason we chose the Statue of Liberty is that since we were children, the Statue has been analogous in our minds with freedom and an America we love."

The commercial possibilities of the statue were always dazzling. Since 1884, when the makers of a popular laxative offered the American Committee $25,000 for the right to inscribe CASTORIA across the top of the pedestal for one year, advertisers have yearned to use the statue as a site for commercials. They have been uniformly turned down by the Park Service, which takes a firm stand against constant requests to permit promotion stunts whether they are commercial, political, or simply bizarre. It once refused a European acrobat who billed himself as "Unus" permission to balance on one finger on Liberty's head.

Nothing, however, can prevent ambitious makers of commercials from using long shots of the statue in whatever way they choose. A Renault automobile was once dangled from a helicopter hovering just off the island, and a 1984 spot for a deodorant shamelessly zeroed in on Liberty's armpit. Such are the uses of freedom.

In 1952, the American Scenic and Historic Preservation Society, whose chairman was then Pierre S. Du Pont III, approached the National Park Service with a proposal to raise funds for and build a museum at the foot of the statue that would record the contribution of immigrants to American life. Although the proposed museum would obscure the bottom of the pedestal with a new concrete-block structure, the Park Service eventually agreed. There was a natural institutional desire to expand the island's facilities, and the vicinity of the statue was obviously a suitable location for an intrinsically good idea. Ellis Island, which might have been even more suitable, was not available. Besides, the plan fitted into a convenient pattern. The Park Service would furnish routine maintenance, transportation, and guide services connected with the museum, while money for construction and large-scale improvements would come, as had the funds for the statue, from privately organized campaigns.

In 1955 the supervising committee, the American Museum of Immigration, Inc., was created. It was headed up by Du Pont, the descendant of eighteenth-century French immigrants, whose little family gunpowder business had grown into a global corporation manufacturing synthetics and chemicals. Other important members included Spyros Skouras, who had come from Greece and made millions as a film exhibitor; George Meany, of blue-collar Irish stock, the president of the AFL-CIO; and Italian immigrant Edward Corsi, a former U.S. Commissioner of Immigration. Back in the 1870s, the figureheads of the French and American statue committees had been academics like Laboulaye and statesmen like Evarts. Indicative of the new world of a century later, the AMI's leaders, Meany and Corsi included, were executives of giant corporations, accustomed to governing through subcommittees, dealing with multimillion-dollar budgets, and directing the work of lobbyists.

The blue-ribbon directorate accumulated enough money to begin construction in 1962, and the doors of the museum opened in 1972. The twenty-year period from idea to inauguration was equal to that required for the statue itself. The museum is impressively organized. It has maps, dioramas, photo-

The Statue of Liberty as seen from Fort Leonard Wood, New Jersey,1948. *Harvey A. Weber, New York.*

FROM MEMORIAL TO SHRINE

graphs, a movie theater, talking exhibits, and tape-recorded interviews with immigrants, immigration officials, and ship captains. It has well-labeled showcases full of memorabilia contributed by immigrants' families—clothes, cooking utensils, farm and craftsmens' tools, furniture, toys, decorations, mementos. It radiates an earnest intention to guard and to exhibit a part of the national heritage as if it were a precious heirloom, no longer in use except on ceremonial occasions. In this it faithfully reflects the spirit of the 1950s. Until then, most Americans had been relentlessly present-minded. Then, newly arrived at world power, they began to feel that they had become separated from their past, which was somehow complete and could be packaged, displayed, admired, and "consumed" as a matter of good citizenship. The statue was a creation. The AMI is a production.

The museum is also in keeping with the gradually evolving program of the Park Service for structuring the experience of visiting a national monument. From the late 1940s it began to arrange exhibits and tours, and provide educational and explanatory material. Some of the changes it made, however, were dictated less by policy than by the growing size of the crowds throughout the 1950s and 1960s. It was difficult to allow as many as eight thousand people, not an unusual total for a pleasant summer Sunday, to mill spontaneously about the island. The total number of visitors in a year exceeded the million mark in 1964 and kept climbing, stopping a little short of two million in the 1980s.

Taking care of such throngs became big business. In 1964 the government contracted with New York's Circle Line to run the ferry service. Twenty years later four new ships were in constant operation; the smallest carries 450 passengers and the largest 1,035. The operating budget for the statue (or, more officially, the Statue of Liberty National Monument) in 1966 was more than $250,000. By the end of the 1970s, a force of twenty-nine uniformed Park Rangers, augmented to forty-five in summertime, was required to shepherd the throngs on and off the ferries and try to keep them from defacing the landscaped grounds or the statue itself. The concession building each week sold multiple thousands of postcards, souvenir ball-point pens, ice-cream bars, hamburgers, and miniatures of the statue.

At the end of 1983, everything came to a temporary halt as work began on a major restoration of the statue in time for its approaching hundredth birthday in 1986.

For a long time, Park Service engineers had been making surveys showing that Liberty had developed serious structural problems. The latest came about in 1980, after two stunting mountaineers made an unauthorized climb up her exterior surfaces. Meanwhile, a group of French enthusiasts for the statue's history had been showing a lively concern for her present-day condition. Various conferences and negotiations spurred by the imminence of the centennial resulted in the formation of a French-American Committee for the Restoration of the Statue of Liberty. Primarily concerned with technical problems, it operates in conjunction with a United States–based fund-raising group, the Statue of Liberty–Ellis Island Foundation. Headed by yet another corporate chief executive, Lee J. Iacocca of the Chrysler Corporation, the Foundation launched a drive in 1982 for a vastly ambitious program. It plans to collect $230 million, not only to restore the statue itself and beautify its surroundings, but also to rehabilitate the crumbling ruins that were once fine buildings on Ellis Island. Some money will be used to cap the job with spectacular festivities.

All through 1984 work continued on the statue, now shrouded in scaffolding and closed to visitors, though they were allowed on Liberty Island if they cared to watch. The planners emphasize that they intend no sharp break with the past. Externally, the statue will look much as she always has, with her emerald patina cleaned but intact. The much-abused flame of the torch has finally gone, and will be replaced with a new one of solid copper, plated with brilliantly reflective gold.

Most of the work will be done on the inside. The weakened internal ribs will be delicately replaced, a few at a time, with hand-molded new ones of corrosion-proof alloy. Thousands of rivets will be replaced; seams and open holes will be plugged with modern, long-lasting sealants. The raised arm, which was not correctly placed in 1886, will be strengthened and a crown spike that rubs against it relocated. The interior of the pedestal will be repainted, air-conditioned, and given a new elevator.

Thierry Despont, a French architect based in New York, heads the reconstruction of the torch of the Statue of Liberty. Despont is shown explaining the deterioration of the statue's face. *AFP/Susan Ragan.*

When it is all done, say the engineers, Liberty will be good for at least another hundred years.

But for all their insistence that she will be the same old statue, there is something about the restoration that sets it apart from the original act of creation a century ago. It is reverent in spirit but high-tech in execution, conducted with strain gauges, X rays of weakened metal parts, computer analyses that work out in seconds problems over which Eiffel must have labored for days. It swallows money in the voracious quantities that the 1980s find customary for projects of any considerable size. Its directors are largely invisible. That is simply the way the world has gone in the last hundred years.

The statue of 1886 was promoted, built, and publicized by strong and distinctive individuals—a liberal scholar, a sculptor, a crusading newspaper editor. When she was finished her head was in the clouds, and her feet in the dirt and casual anarchy of an unsupervised Bedloe's Island. She was like the humanity she was meant to enlighten.

Swathed in scaffolding the Statue of Liberty undergoes extensive renovation inside and out. *Jeffrey D. Smith, Woodfin Camp & Associates.*

Above and right:

Borglum's defective old torch will be replaced with a new one of solid copper and brilliant gold plate. The arm, incorrectly placed at the time of the statue's erection, will be shifted, and a spike that formerly chafed against it will be moved. *Jet Lowe/Historic American Engineering Record.*

Corrosion to the face and exterior will be repaired. *Jet Lowe/ Historic American Engineering Record.*

The "restored" statue of 1986 and after will not have that kind of imprint or setting. In her well-scrubbed, tidily arranged, thoroughly explicated surroundings, she may have a bit more of the look of a treasure kept in an invisible, gargantuan glass case.

And yet it is doubtful that preservation will deprive her of the uncanny power she has always had to create a sense of one-to-one relationship between herself and individual Americans. It's a power vividly evoked by a newspaper reporter who, in 1984, interviewed construction workers as they nursed their coffee cups, waiting for the 7:30 A.M. ferry to take them to their jobs. They all referred to the statue as "the Lady." "To me, the job is a little special," said one, an Italian immigrant. "I come from the other side." An electrician declared: "This is something you want to do. She is all ours for a while." A blacksmith working on molds of the ribs said: "I guess, whether we admit it or not, we are all in love with her." Bob Conmy, a member of the scaffolding crew, did not have to say anything. He was one of the first to reach the level of the statue's face and look her in her enormous eye. He leaned forward and gave her a kiss.

Reactions like that cannot be programmed. Nor are they created by a century of ceremonies and speechmaking. People who say they are in love with "the Lady" have not read the speeches. They simply know her as a live presence. Whatever their individual definitions of freedom, or America, or both together may be, the statue gives them articulation, soul, and feeling.

Bartholdi built a goddess of liberty, with a classic, imposing stride and posture. But she became a goddess with whom her devotees feel very much at home. The birthday celebration that seems most typical of her is not the star-studded fiftieth, but the eightieth, on October 29, 1966. On that day, the Ladies' Auxiliary of the Veterans of Foreign Wars presented Superintendent Lester McClanahan with a $2,500 check raised by the membership for the purpose of planting trees on Liberty Island. Mrs. Glenn C. White of South Bend, Indiana, the chairman of the Auxiliary, wore a smashing purple outfit. The St. Mary's High School Band of Rutherford, New Jersey, played *Mademoiselle from Armentières* and *Give My Regards to Broadway*.

That is the image that lingers. That and construction worker Bob Conmy planting an enthusiastic, irreverent buss on Liberty's copper head. Frédéric Auguste Bartholdi, Emma Lazarus, and Joseph Pulitzer would almost certainly have approved.

A **workman kisses** the Statue of Liberty as renovation begins, in 1984. © *1985 Koni Nordmann/Contact Press Images.*

U·S·A BONDS
Third Liberty Loan Campaign
BOY SCOUTS OF AMERICA
Be prepared
WEAPONS FOR LIBERTY

CHAPTER SIX

THE INDELIBLE IMAGE

Not even the best friends of the Statue of Liberty can claim that it belongs among the mightiest works of Western art. Bartholdi was no Michelangelo. In his own time, he was thought of as a rather academic sculptor, far inferior to contemporaries like Rodin. Even Marvin Trachtenberg, an art historian who has written a thoroughly admiring study of the statue, says that "most of Bartholdi's work shows hardly a trace of originality."

And yet the mighty woman with the torch is probably the best-known piece of sculpture in America, instantly recognizable to millions completely unfamiliar with the classics displayed in the world's museums. The statue's image has steadily grown in familiarity in the past hundred years; and it is now universally known and almost as universally admired. If it is not a masterpiece it is, beyond quarrel, a towering success.

What accounts for this enduring appeal?

One answer may be found in a remark by critic Harold Rosenberg: the Statue of Liberty is a monument, and "the things that are important in a work of art and in a monument are not necessarily the same." The statue belongs with creations that become mythological. It is not to be compared with museum pieces.

Right from the start remarkable dimensions made the statue a celebrity—the world's tallest—a modern wonder in a wonder-filled new world. But it outlasted that temporary glory, which vanished as more imposing gigantic structures were built, and took on other and more durable roles. First, Liberty became the mother of exiles. And then, with the government's propaganda campaigns in World War I, the statue became *the* figure immediately identifiable as America, first joining and then more or less displacing Uncle Sam and "Columbia." Originally it had suggested Franco-American friendship and international peace. Now it became "Americanized," a process that had deep repercussions on how often and in what light it was portrayed. In the United States, the statue was treated with a strange, democratic mixture of veneration and easygoing familiarity—a goddess on one hand, and an image as popular as a comic-strip heroine or a movie star on the other. It became something of a media figure in a society that the media were learning to dominate. In the world at large, it came to stand for "the American way" in all its implications, at a time when America emerged as a superpower and self-proclaimed worldwide defender of the non-Communist world.

But above all, the statue's perseverance in our minds rests on the solid foundation of the ideal that it originally was meant to embody—Liberty. It represents all of liberty's powerful and sometimes clashing definitions. And because it is such a universal aspiration, with such a multitude of meanings, the statue, as its symbol, speaks to an unlimited audience. The image may be glorified, stylized, interpreted and reinterpreted, parodied. In whatever guise, it awakens strong sentiments, rarely indifference. And so the statue has a special place in the "iconographic vocabulary" of each of us.

USA Bonds—Weapons for Liberty. J. C. Leyendecker designed this poster celebrating the Boy Scouts and the role they played in the third Liberty Bond campaign. *Statue of Liberty National Monument, New York.*

Save Your Child. Liberty's hand and torch stood for the whole statue in Herbert Paus's poster for War Savings Stamps, available in smaller denominations than War Bonds. *Statue of Liberty National Monument, New York.*

Bottom:

Liberty...Beloved Liberty... Poster by Natacha Carlu for the Free French Press and Information Service, 1940. *Statue of Liberty National Monument, New York.*

Opposite:

To the glory of the French and **American armies.** Fabric designed during World War I to commemorate ties between the two nations. *Cooper-Hewitt Museum, The Smithsonian Institution's National Museum of Design, New York.*

America, America: The Heroic Portrait

From the earliest days of the fund-raising drives for the statue it has, for the most part, enjoyed a positive image. The majority of representations aim at its glorification. The statue is most familiar to us in a heroic stance. It can be the spirit of freedom and progress, receiving the homage of nations, as in Edward Moran's early, misty portraits. Though they look creditably authentic, they are an entirely imaginary view of how Liberty looks on her pedestal, since they were done for the French Committee before the statue was actually inaugurated.

Liberty can raise her torch protectively over the diverse American populace, as she does in photographs and posters and in popular spectacles like *Miss Liberty*. Or she can be a resolute and embattled America, calling on her children for sacrifices, as in the propaganda effusions of both world wars. Sometimes, as in the trophy given by Pulitzer to Bartholdi in 1886, the torch alone is enough to invoke the meaning of the entire statue.

Liberty is also effectively used in patriotic partnership with other American figures—the Founding Fathers, the American eagle, or the flag. This is especially evident in a familiar but minor art form with which most of us have daily contact—postage stamps. It is not surprising to Americans to find a regal and inspiring Statue of Liberty on any number of United States postage stamps—either alone or in some honorific combination with American servicemen, Boy Scouts, and air mail pilots. But it is something of a pleasant reminder of America's message to the world to find Liberty's torch casting its rays over various multicolored backgrounds on the stamps of at least two dozen other nations.

More than a hundred stamps from at least twenty-four countries have featured the statue. *Musée de la Poste, Paris.*

MAKE AMERICA A BETTER PLACE.

LEAVE THE COUNTRY.

Of all the ways America can grow, one way is by learning from others.

There are things you can learn in the Peace Corps you can't learn anywhere else.

You could start an irrigation program. And find that crabgrass and front lawns look a little ridiculous. When there isn't enough wheat to go around in Nepal.

You could be the outsider who helps bring a Jamaican fishing village to life, for the first time in three hundred years. And you could wonder if your country has outsiders enough. In Watts. In Detroit. In Appalachia. On its Indian reservations.

Last year, for the first time, Peace Corps alumni outnumbered Volunteers who are now out at work overseas.

By 1980, 200,000 Peace Corps alumni will be living their lives in every part of America.

There are those who think you can't change the world in the Peace Corps.

On the other hand, maybe it's not just what you do in the Peace Corps that counts.

But what you do when you get back.
The Peace Corps, Washington, D.C. 20525. ⓐ

ADVERTISING CONTRIBUTED FOR THE PUBLIC GOOD

Opposite:

Liberty Gun. Ink drawing by Michel Guiré-Vaka, 1970. Liberty has exchanged her attributes for those of imperialism. *Collection of the artist, Paris.*

Top left:

Planet of the Apes. Final sequence of the 1968 Franklin J. Schaffner movie, produced by Twentieth Century Fox. *Collection of Christophe L., Paris.*

Bottom left:

Petrified New York. Acrylic by Jean Lagarrigue, 1968. The illustration appeared in *Esquire* with an article on the future of America. *Collection of the artist, Paris.*

Top:

The Third World Demands a Larger Share of the Riches. Pen and ink drawing by Piem illustrating an article about a meeting of non-aligned nations, 1981. *APEI Press Agency, Paris.*

Bottom left:

I Wash My Hands of Them. Pen and ink drawing by Piem illustrating an article on the Cambodian boat people. *APEI Press Agency, Paris.*

Bottom, center:

The Camp David Accords. Pen and ink drawing by Piem, 1978. *APEI Press Agency, Paris.*

Far left:

Khomeini. Drawing by Jacques Faizant, 1979. The Iranian religious leader sets the torch to Liberty. *Collection of the artist, Paris.*

Left:

Untitled drawing in India ink by Mordillo, 1968. *Collection of the artist, Paris.*

THE INDELIBLE IMAGE

"OK, YOU HUDDLED MASSES. I KNOW YOU'RE IN HERE."

Top:

Immigration Reform. Pen and ink drawing by John Trever, 1981. *Courtesy of the "Albuquerque Journal."*

Sweeps of Aliens OKd. Pen and ink drawing by Signe Wilkinson, 1984. *Courtesy of the "San Jose Mercury-News."*

The Statue's Rub-Off Magic

Almost from the beginning of the struggle to raise the money to build the statue, Bartholdi recognized that his visualization of Liberty somehow enormously enhanced any commercial message. He hurried to copyright the statue in France and the United States so he could control and profit by the rights of reproduction of the image. Temporarily he transferred his rights to the promotion committees, so that businessmen who wanted to put Liberty behind their products had to pay into the building funds. He hoped once the statue was complete and in place, royalties would be all his. He was, however, the victim of his own success. Despite his threats to prosecute unauthorized users of the statue's image, by 1886 it was already so well known and widely copied that as a practical matter he could not enforce his rights.

The statue has been used to sell just about everything. Many of the reproductions of the statue's image are simple souvenir gimcrackery. Yet in spite of constant reappearance in somewhat tawdry or at least commonplace settings, the statue retains the peculiar power of lending credibility and dignity not merely to products that swarm in the marketplace but to ideas, to causes, and even to individuals and institutions. It seems entirely and appropriately in place to draw attention to the Peace Corps or the plight of Soviet Jews, or to a wall mural celebrating the International Year of Women. But it pops up as well in other, oddly assorted but not totally illogical places—on a medal commemorating the flight of two French aviators from Paris to New York, the sheet music of a song popularized by Maurice Chevalier, a stained-glass window in the Columbia School of Journalism endowed by Joseph Pulitzer, a decorative watchcase celebrating the Wright brothers.

There is a kind of transferable "clout" in the image that has proven perennially attractive, sometimes leading to bizarre expressions of admiration. There was apparently a vogue, at one time, for people to dress up and pose as the statue. And then there is imitation, the sincerest form of flattery. There are a number of reproductions of the statue in France[1]—and there was once one in Hanoi. In 1901 a New York warehouse owner proudly placed a replica of the statue on the roof, where it still stands.[2] And as late as the 1950s, the Boy Scouts of America distributed a number of replicas throughout the United States.

Label for a crate of California pears, 1927. *Private Collection, Paris.*

Holland-America Line poster by Mettes for the famous transatlantic liner the SS *Nieuw Amsterdam*, 1955. *Bibliothèque Forney, Paris.*

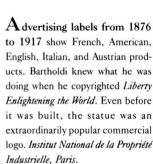

Advertising labels from 1876 to 1917 show French, American, English, Italian, and Austrian products. Bartholdi knew what he was doing when he copyrighted *Liberty Enlightening the World*. Even before it was built, the statue was an extraordinarily popular commercial logo. *Institut National de la Propriété Industrielle, Paris.*

Right:

Kent cigarettes. Poster by Michel Dubré for Kent's European market. *Collection of the artist, Paris.*

Far right:

WNBC Radio. The statue dominates all of the great symbols of New York. *Statue of Liberty National Monument, New York.*

Bottom:

Loïs jeans. Advertisement by Michel Dubré, 1981. Liberty in a surreal American landscape. *Private Collection, Paris.*

KENT. LA CIGARETTE U.S. INTERNATIONALE

WNBC Radio 66

...SUR SES JEANS ÉTAIT MARQUÉ LOÍS!

Lois JEANS & JACKETS

The Statue as Inspiration to Artists

The statue has naturally been a source of inspiration to artists and photographers, who, in one way or another have rendered it in accordance with their particular schools and styles. Thus it can appear charmingly and conventionally in a 1976 painting entitled *New York 1904* and done in something of a 1904 style. But recognizable and strongly individualistic modern artists have adapted it to their own stylistic messages. Roy Lichtenstein does it as something of a comic-strip panel; Andy Warhol repeats its image over and over in the kind of sequence that he made famous with Campbell's Soup cans; Peter Max's rendition is in his recognizable bright colors and swirling lines that flow into each other in what looks like sweetly childlike fashion; and Pol Bury subjects it, through a special graphic technique, to a series of zany distortions that make it look as if it were posing before a fun-house mirror.

Whether Bury's aim is forthrightly to kid the statue is not clear, but it is clearly a subject for jokes that rely on putting its familiar features in a novel context. That is the beauty of familiarity; we need only the suggestion of an upraised torch or a cradled tablet to awaken whatever responses Liberty awakens in us— and then the artist can play with those responses by changing details. Liberty can become a waitress offering breakfast, a Coca-Cola bottle, an apple-eating onlooker at New York Harbor—or whatever fancy dictates. Cartoonists and photographers can also play games involving us and the statue. Sometimes the point is a little obscure—as in the rendition of the statue, transformed into a man, holding up a lighted match against a small forest of them—and sometimes, as when the statue becomes Mae West or the Marx Brothers, it is abundantly clear. Whether you think such caricatures are innocent merriment or signify the breakdown of respect for American institutions, the fact remains that what makes them "work" is the permanent presence of the statue in our consciousness. It is the foundation on which all representations of it are built.

In whatever form—heroine, victim, butt of satire, drumbeater for national or commercial causes—the Statue of Liberty's image remains strong, recognizable, and permanent. Conventional artist or not, Bartholdi wrought something special, and he knew it.

New York, 1904. Acrylic by Yves Méry, 1976. The arrival in the United States after the ocean crossing. *Collection of the artist, Paris.*

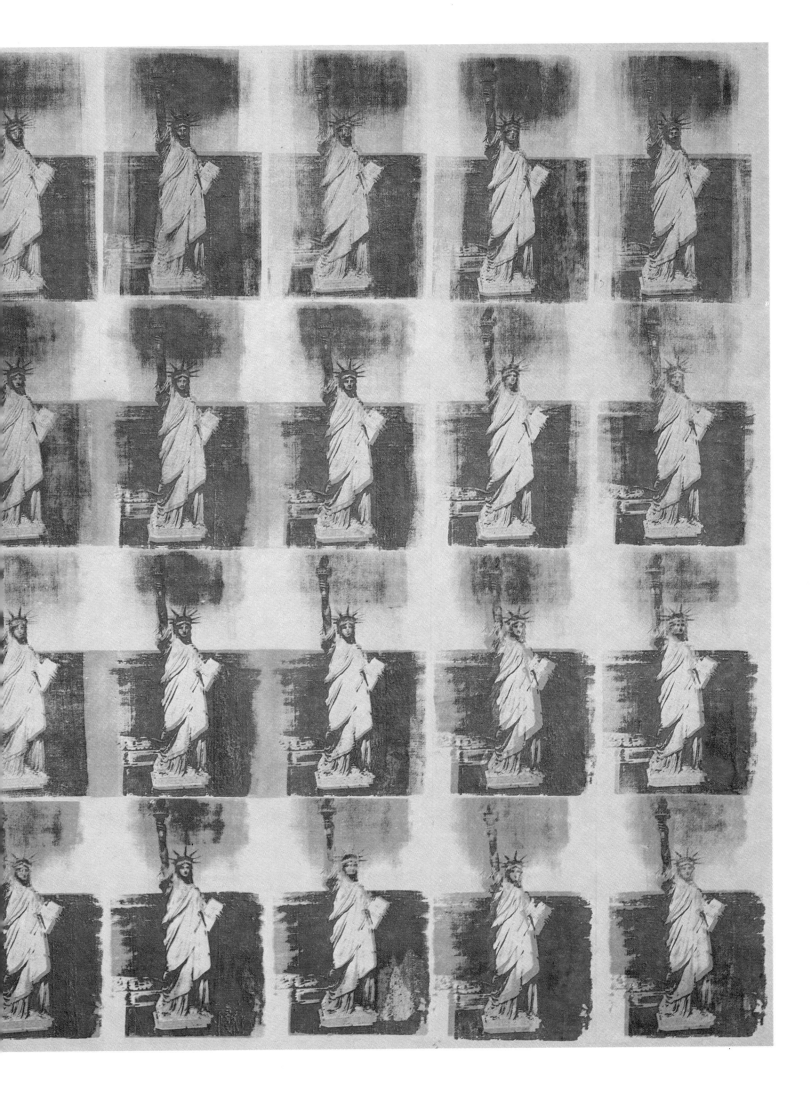

Right:

ixer. Mixed media by Pol Bury, 1972. The artist imagined the statue as a series of horizontal sections: manipulating the central skeleton would produce wildly different distortions of the familiar form. *Collection of the artist, Paris.*

Opposite:

Statue of Liberty. Acrylic on canvas by Peter Max. Paintings presented to President Reagan at the White House on July 4, 1981. *Collection of the artist, New York.*

Peter Max 1981 —
Statue of Liberty —
Painted at The White House July 4, 1981

Peter Max 1981 —
Statue of Liberty —
Painted at The White House July 4, 1981

Peter Max 1981 —
Statue of Liberty —
Painted at The White House July 4, 1981

Peter Max 1981 —
Statue of Liberty —
Painted at The White House July 4, 1981

Portrait of Auguste Bartholdi painted by Jean Brenner. *Bartholdi Museum, Colmar.*

B I O G R A P H Y

1834 August 2. Birth, in Colmar, France, of Frédéric-Auguste Bartholdi. Son of Jean-Charles Bartholdi and Auguste-Charlotte Beysser. The Bartholdis, married in 1829, belonged to the Protestant bourgeoisie of Alsace. They had their first son, Charles, in 1831.

1836 Death of Jean-Charles Bartholdi. His widow is thirty-five years old; Frédéric-Auguste, two. The family leaves Colmar and takes up residence in Paris. Frédéric-Auguste enters a lycée there and is a mediocre student but shows an early aptitude for drawing.

1847 Bartholdi frequents the Paris studios of the sculptor Antoine Etex (creator of the bas-relief *La Résistance* on the Arc de Triomphe), the painter Ary Scheffer, a friend of the family, and the sculptor Jean-François Soitoux.

1853 At nineteen, Bartholdi presents a sculpted group titled *The Good Samaritan at the Salon* and receives his first commission from Colmar—a statue of General Rapp, a local hero and aide-de-camp to Napoleon I. Eleven and one half feet tall on a fourteen-foot pedestal, the monument was presented at the Universal Exposition in 1855 where it was noticed by the press. It would be inaugurated in 1856. Bartholdi proposes to the municipality of Colmar a monument to the memory of Admiral Bruat, another local man who distinguished himself during the Crimean War.
    Bartholdi travels to Egypt where he is strongly impressed by the colossal statues.

1857 The city of Bordeaux holds a design competition for a monumental fountain. Bartholdi enters and wins first prize. This fountain would be built thirty years later in Lyons.

1859 Bartholdi works on a monumental fountain combining architecture and sculpture in Marseille.

1864 Completion of a monument honoring the martyrs of Poland. Inauguration in Colmar of the statue of Admiral Bruat.

1865 Bartholdi meets Edouard de Laboulaye and takes part in liberal republican meetings at his house in Glatigny.

1866 Bartholdi makes a terra-cotta bust of Laboulaye.

1867-68 He works on the first model of a lighthouse for the entrance to the Suez Canal, *Progress Bringing Light to Asia.*

1869 Opening of the Suez Canal. Bartholdi draws a study of the monument for Ismail Pasha, Viceroy of Egypt. It would never be built.

1870 Bartholdi makes the first signed and dated model of *Liberty Enlightening the World*. He makes a model for his statue *Vercingétorix* for the village of Clermont-Ferrand.
    On July 19, France declares war on Prussia. Bartholdi joins the national guard. He is put in charge of organizing the defense of Colmar and, after the fall of the city, is named aide-de-camp to Giuseppe Garibaldi, the Italian fighter who volunteered to help the French Republic.

1871 On May 10, the Treaty of Paris is signed at Versailles, ceding Alsace-Lorraine to Prussia. Bartholdi travels to the United States.

1872 He begins a statue of Lafayette ordered by the French community in New York. It would later be offered by the French government to the City of New York.

1874 Bartholdi designs four bas-reliefs for the Brattle Street Church in Boston (which would become the First Baptist Church). They represent the four stages of Christian life: Baptism, Communion, Marriage, and Death.

1875 He executes a fountain for the Philadelphia Exposition. Later it was moved to the Botanical Garden in Washington, D.C.

1876 Bartholdi makes a trip to the United States with the French Commission to the Universal Exposition in Philadelphia. Presentation of the hand and torch of the Statue of Liberty in Philadelphia and then in Madison Square, New York, where it would remain until 1881. Inauguration of the statue of Lafayette in Union Square, New York.
  On December 29, Bartholdi marries Jeanne-Emilie Baheux de Puysieux in Newport, Rhode Island.

1878 Presentation of the head of the Statue of Liberty at the Universal Exposition in Paris, and inauguration of the statue of Lafayette in Paris.

1880 Bartholdi completes the *Lion of Belfort*, works on bas-reliefs for the Theatre des Arts in Rouen, and makes a terra-cotta bust of William Evarts, secretary of state and president of the American Committee for the Statue of Liberty.

1884 Bartholdi executes a statue of the encyclopedist Denis Diderot for the city of Langres.

1885 A second version of the fountain made for the Philadelphia Exposition is erected in Rheims.
  Erection in Paris of a reduction of the Statue of Liberty, paid for by the American community in Paris.
  On May 22, the Statue of Liberty is put aboard the *Isère* for the trip to America, where Bartholdi would go for a short stay in October.

1886 October 28, inauguration of the Statue of Liberty in New York.

1887 A replica of the Statue of Liberty is erected in Hanoi, and a reduction of it is placed in a fountain in Bordeaux.

1888 Inauguration of Bartholdi's Roesselmann Fountain, in Colmar.

1889 A reduction of the Statue of Liberty is placed on the western tip of the Ile des Cygnes in Paris.

1891 Inauguration of a monument to the republican leader Léon Gambetta in Ville-d'Avray.

1892 Bartholdi works on Joseph Pulitzer's commission for a monument to Lafayette and Washington for Paris.

1895 The Lafayette and Washington monument is inaugurated in Paris.

1904 Bartholdi dies in Paris, October 5.

(This biography does not list all of Bartholdi's works.)

The Bartholdi Fountain.
Engraving of a fountain completed by
the sculptor in 1876 and placed in
Washington's Botanical Gardens. A
replica may be found in Reims. *Private Collection, Paris.*

I BIRTH OF A SYMBOL

1. Built between 1882 and 1884, the viaduct at Garabit is 1,861 feet long. At its highest point, it arches 492 feet above the river.

2. The exact length is 5,989 feet.

3. The first universal exposition opened in London in 1855, followed by one in Paris in 1867 and another in Philadelphia in 1876.

4. Using the same technique, Phidias made the nearly forty-foot statue of Athena Parthenos in gold and ivory, and the sixty-foot Athena Promachos in bronze. Deinocrates's even more ambitious plan, that of sculpting out of Mount Athos a seated representation of Alexander the Great, was never carried out. The Romans also built a large number of colossal statues. The one-hundred-and-seventeen-foot statue of Nero by Zenodore is the most famous.

For all of our material on colossal statues we are indebted to Marvin Trachtenberg's excellent study *Statue of Liberty*; Charles Talensier's article "La Statue de la Liberté Éclairant le Monde"; *Les plus grandes entreprises du monde* by Daniel Bellet and William Darville; and Maurice Agulhon's article "La Statue de la Liberté," all of which are listed in the Bibliography.

5. Legend has it that it was placed at the entrance to the harbor, one foot on either side of the channel. But this is impossible since the passage through the legs, estimated according to the statue's height, would not have been large enough to allow ships to pass. Although it was filled with stones to assure stability, it fell over in an earthquake about fifty years after it was erected. It remained in that sad condition for nearly nine hundred years.

6. Letter from Bartholdi to Laboulaye, July 15, 1871: "Up to now, as far as the project goes, I still don't have anything final. I could probably only lay out the roughest outlines; as I learn more about my site I'll do more, but these rough ideas may end up not just a monument but a work of a greater moral value."

7. For the rest of his life Bartholdi had to defend himself against two attacks concerning the origin of the work. The first was that it was the "personal whim of the artist." It is certain from the body of his work that the idea of a colossal statue was his, and his sketches for Suez were sufficiently far along to prove it. He himself said in 1885, "I can honestly claim a certain amount of credit for thinking up the idea, carrying it out, and seeing it through to completion." That he was obliged to give it a wider significance stems from his own strong feelings or those of the people who commissioned the work.

The second complaint was that the idea was not original enough —that Liberty was essentially a recycling of his idea for a lighthouse for the Suez Canal. When he was attacked in 1884 by American newspapers opposed to the acceptance of a secondhand gift, Bartholdi claimed that he had made only one small terra-cotta statuette for Ismail Pasha, and that there was no resemblance between *Progress* and *Liberty* except that both were lighthouses in the form of a woman holding a torch. He went on to explain that it was difficult for a sculptor to "hide his light under her skirts or a bushel." Bartholdi never mentioned the other statuettes of *Progress* he made, which still exist today. And as for having to put the light in the torch, in Bartholdi's early studies for *Progress* and *Liberty*, the light came not from the torch but from the crown.

The inspiration for *Liberty* is evident, as is her resemblance to *Progress*. Bartholdi should not have had to apologize for borrowing from himself.

8. The *Courier des États Unis*, November 25, 1875, reports that "the *Times* expressed the hope that the artist won't cap Liberty with a Phrygian bonnet," and stated further that "without sharing the ridiculous antipathy of the prefect of the Côte d'Or, who had a statue wearing the emblem brutally torn down and destroyed, we would say frankly that to our taste, the most beautiful ornament for a woman's head is her hair without any accessory. We know the Phrygian bonnet is known to all, and that it would have the advantage of immediately indicating the significance of the statue. But the genius of the sculptor should be able to make Liberty recognizable by the character of her features and her attitude."

9. "Moreover, this revolutionary Liberty cannot evoke American liberty, which, after a hundred years of uninterrupted existence, should appear not as an intrepid young girl but as a woman of mature years, calm, advancing with the light but sure step of progress. She should emphasize the Order of establishing rather than the Order of tearing down." Bartholdi, *The Statue of Liberty Enlightening the World*.

10. The tablets of the Law were a late addition. The medal of the first subscription by the Franco-American Union (September 1875) shows Liberty holding broken chains.

11. Not only would bronze casting require the assembling of many parts. Because of the contraction of the metal, the joints between parts would be clearly noticeable. Moreover, quick calculations would dismiss the possibility altogether. More than fifty-two feet high, the bronze Virgin of Puy weighed nearly one hundred tons. The Statue of Liberty would weigh three times as much, and its pedestal would thus have to be huge in relation to the size of the statue. Instead Bartholdi chose the copper repoussé technique used for the San Carlo Borromeo. Rolled and hammered copper provided an unbeatable weight-to-volume ratio, assuring solidity, lightness, and longevity superior to that of cast copper.

12. An interior armature, or skeleton, was necessary because the lightweight copper plates would not offer sufficient resistance to the wind. Ordinarily in hollow statues, the spaces between the interior armature and the outer envelope were filled with stonework. When repairs were needed, everything had to be demolished—which would have been impossible in the case of Liberty. Viollet-le-Duc had conceived of a system of internal compartments filled with sand, so that when repairs were needed, it would be enough to empty the sand out of one compartment to leave room for the repairman. See Charles Blanc, *Le Temps*, March 27, 1878.

---

2 FROM SHORE TO SHORE

1. "All the liberal press supports us very warmly here, we have every reason to hope for a great success. Supporters arrive in droves, we have plenty of signatures; at the same time, there's a danger that the country, tired out by its charitable works, won't come up with all the money we may need. Would it not be possible, sir, to organize in New York a committee corresponding to ours which, getting in touch with the French community and other cities, would help us to raise the necessary funds for our patriotic work, which, because of its colossal size, will be very expensive. We are counting on the patriotism of all French people, adopted citizens of the United States, and we hope to see them join in our grand enterprise." In *Le Courrier des États Unis*, November 13, 1875.

2. "The great industrialists have had the honor of generously showing their patriotism. A great number of them have circulated lists in their factories where they've gotten large numbers of signatures. Our business community, which has numerous ties to the U.S., is showing the value it attaches to this demonstration of peace and friendship between the two peoples. The chambers of commerce, the municipal councils, the principal cities of France have already voted subscriptions. Others are announcing their own drives, and it is likely that this movement will continue, because all our cities must want in their hearts to be represented on the rosters of this patriotic gesture." In *Le Siècle*, November 28, 1875, and *Le Bien Public*, November 29, 1875.

3. To support the effort, the list of subscribers was published throughout December, especially the names of those who seemed the most inventive. There was, for example, the American aerialist Rufus Gibbon Wells, who gave the committee the funds he received from his stunts.

4. Beginning at eight o'clock all of Paris's Americans and Americanophiles crowded the ticket window but they were not enough to fill the room. Of the twenty-two thousand francs that a sold-out performance could earn, the day's receipts were only 8,291 francs, barely enough to cover costs. The *National*, even though it approved of what the committee was doing, wrote in its review, "The performance was a little long." *Le Figaro* ended its April 26 article: "I recommend to you one song they sang last night, titled 'On the Ramparts.' You expect something patriotic, isn't that so? Well, here are the lyrics, word for word: 'Let us drink, let us sing,/In this sweet intoxication we'll look for true happiness. Friends, keep singing for honor and country.' This mixture of country, honor, and *petit bleu* made a singular impression. The event ended with 'Hail Columbia,' America's national anthem. And we left, sadly, with an envious glance at the representatives of the American colony. They, at least, had just suffered for their country."

5. "If the French send us a statue," wrote the *Times* in November 1875, "this would be a work which would do credit to their taste as well as to their affectionate sentiments....That the statue would be a

Bartholdi and his mother. A photograph. *Bartholdi Museum, Colmar.*

Rouget de L'Isle. Engraving of a sculpture by Bartholdi for the city of Laons-le-Saulnier in 1882. Published in *Le Journal Illustré*, July 23, 1882. *Bibliothèque Forney, Paris.*

Fountain pen. *Collection Lacroux, Paris.*

respectable work of art is not to be doubted. The men who have the business in hand cannot be suspected of practicing artistic ideas that one would ordinarily find in the committees of Congress. They should be touched by the confidence that our public places in their wisdom. If it were Congress that had decided to put up a colossal statue in our harbor, intelligent New Yorkers would turn pale with worry. They would hasten to sell everything they own in New York and escape to the countryside. We are spared such a calamity."

6. Bartholdi wrote to Laboulaye on October 10: "I think that the last newspapers that I had the pleasure of sending you will have reassured you somewhat about the future of the work of the French-American Union. My stay here already has been longer than I expected and I am obliged to stay on, but I think I can guarantee now that whatever happens to our subscription in France, the project will be carried out and with enthusiasm. The setbacks, the late arrival of the arm, and everything which has gone wrong are the sole causes of the delay. At the present time, if we wanted to put the statue in Philadelphia, we would find all the necessary funds, but this wouldn't be the same thing."

7. Certain pieces were numbered incorrectly, which created difficulties when the statue was erected in New York. The rivets, washers, and bolts alone filled thirty-six crates.

---

3 TOWARD THE NEW WORLD

1. The Committee met at the Union League Club November 22, 1881. Evarts himself wrote to Laboulaye: "I assure you, my dear Monsieur Laboulaye, that we have no doubt our countrymen will joyfully provide the money for the pedestal and that we will be able to finish building it in time for it to receive the noble statue which your genius and generosity have offered us." André de Laboulaye, "La Statue de la Liberté," *Franco-American Review*, 1938. For his part, Hunt got in touch with Bartholdi, who informed Butler on December 25: "I've received a letter from Hunt, the architect, asking for specifications concerning the pedestal. I'm rushing to supply them to him at the same time that I forward the drawings and calculations of our engineers, extremely important papers that we'll have to take good care of and show to experienced people to study so that they can decide how to anchor the statue to the pedestal. I mentioned our ideas on the architectural look of the monument—he'll probably tell you about them."

2. After the debacle at Ball's Bluff, October 21, 1861, the public wanted a scapegoat, and Stone, an inexperienced brigadier-general, was close at hand. He was accused of incompetence and treason, arrested, and put in prison at Fort Lafayette in New York Harbor, where he spent fifty days in solitary confinement trying to find out the charges against him. It took an act of Congress to release him in August 1862. His work on the Statue of Liberty brought him back to familiar territory, under more favorable circumstances.

3. The description of the contents of the box varied from one newspaper to another. It is supposed to have contained a copy of the U.S. Constitution, a copy of the Declaration of Independence, a copy of Washington's farewell address to his troops, a bronze medal in honor of Washington dated 1776, nineteen bronze medals representing the Presidents since Washington, a medal commemorating the erection of the Egyptian obelisk in Central Park, an almanac for 1884, a list of French members of the New York State Masonic

Lodge, a portrait of Bartholdi, a copy of the financial report on the statue, visiting cards of those present, a half dollar showing Lafayette on one side and Washington on the other, copies of newspapers from the day before, and a copy of the Statutes of the Sons of the Revolution.

4. A special railway was built to carry the stones to the harbor.

5. According to the *Congressional Record* of July 2, 1886, Hewitt broke down the expenses in the following manner:

Installing the statue, according to H. F. Spaulding, treasurer of the American Committee	$15,000
Construction of viewing stands for the inauguration, decoration, music, police	3,520
Refreshments for approx. 500 guests	2,500
Last-minute expenses	480
Reception for the French officials	9,000
Cleaning the island, removing unsightly buildings, erecting the stands	5,000
Construction of a new dock	16,000
Installing electricity	15,000
Interior elevator in fort	7,200
Covered walkways between the walls of the fort and the foundations of the pedestal	26,400
	$106,100

It should be noted that the total is really $100,100, rather than $106,100. No one in the House or Senate noticed the error. As a result the two houses, having decided to subtract several items to reduce the budget, arrived at a final budget of $57,300 which still included this $6,000. Thus six thousand dollars escaped the vigilance of Congress.

---

5 FROM MEMORIAL TO SHRINE

1. Though the Statue of Liberty National Monument is federally owned, is it located in New Jersey or in New York State? The question is practical as well as theoretical, since it involves the right to collect sales taxes at the concession stands. New Jersey advocates like to note that Bedloe's (now Liberty) Island is in New Jersey waters, closer to Jersey City than to Manhattan, and listed on Jersey City real estate tax rolls. Moreover, the Statue's electric power and water come from New Jersey. Unfortunately for their argument, an 1834 agreement between the two states gives New York all those parts of the island above the mean low-water mark—leaving New Jersey with only the riparian rights to all submerged land surrounding the Statue.

---

6 THE INDELIBLE IMAGE

1. Offered in 1884 by the American community in Paris, it was initially erected in the Place des Etats Unis before being transferred for the 1889 Universal Exposition to the Ile des Cygnes, where it is located today. For the Exposition, the statue faced east, toward Paris, according to the wish of the president of the Republic. Since then, it has been turned to face west, toward its American sister.

2. The versions in Bordeaux and Hanoi have disappeared. In New York City, a miniature version still exists on the roof of a building belonging to the Liberty Storage and Warehouse Company.

B I B L I O G R A P H Y

Books

Agulhon, Maurice. *"La statue de la Liberté."* In *La révolution américaine et l'Europe*, Colloques internationaux du Centre National de la Recherche Scientifique, no. 577. Paris: CNRS, 1979.

Bartholdi, Auguste. *Album de bord: Galerie des portraits authentiques des membres du jury français et de leurs compagnons embarqués sur et pour l'Amérique, exécuté sur le gaillard d'arrière. Expurgée, revue et augmentée après avoir consulté les originaux.* Paris: Bartholdi, Simonin, Fouret et Cie, 1879.

_____*The Statue of Liberty Enlightening the World Described by the Sculptor...Published for the Benefit of the Pedestal Fund.* New York: North American Review, 1885.

Bellet, Daniel, and William Darville. *Les plus grandes entreprises du monde.* Paris: Flammarion, n.d.

Betz, Jacques. *Bartholdi.* Paris: Editions de Minuit, 1954.

Bigot, Charles. *De Paris au Niagara: Journal de voyage d'une délégation.* Paris: A. Dupret, 1887.

Browne, Anita, ed. *Golden Jubilee Poems of the Statue of Liberty...Compiled from the Poetry Contest Sponsored by the National Life Conservation Society in Co-operation with the National Park Service of the United States.* New York: The Poet Press, 1936.

Butler, Nicolas Murray. *Address at the Dinner Commemorating the Dedication of the Statue of Liberty, Hotel Waldorf Astoria.* October 28, 1936.

Canu, Jean. *Histoire des Etats-Unis.* Colloques *Que sais-je?* Paris: P.U.F., 1941.

Cossart, Michael de. *Une Américaine à Paris.* Paris: Librairie Plon, 1979.

Depew, Chauncey Mitchell. *Oration by the Hon. C. M. Depew at the Unveiling of Bartholdi's Statue of Liberty Enlightening the World.* New York: The De Vinne Press, 1886.

Deswarte, Sylvie, and Raymond Guidot. *Historique de la Statue de la Liberté.* Paris: Centre de Création Industrielle, Centre Georges Pompidou, 1976.

Finlasson, Eric C. *The Statue of Liberty.* London: Quality Press, 1942.

Giclas, Louis. *Album of Light. Arguments for Respect to Public Monuments.* Washington: 1924.

_____*The Beautiful Necessity.* Washington: 1929.

_____*The Conscript of 1917: How to View the Beacon and Political Art.* New York: 1934.

Gilder, Rodman. *Statue of Liberty Enlightening the World.* New York: The New York Trust Co., 1943.

Gontrand, Reinhard et Cie. *Album des travaux de construction de la Statue Colossale de la Liberté.* Paris: 1888.

Gschaedler, André. *True Light on the Statue of Liberty and Its Creator.* Narberth, Pa.: Livingston Publishing Co., 1966.

Handlin, Oscar, and the editors of the book division. *Statue of Liberty.* New York: Newsweek, 1971.

Horwitz, Elinor Lander, and J. Roderick Moore. *The Bird, the Banner and Uncle Sam.* Philadelphia and New York: J. B. Lippincott Co., 1976.

Kennedy, John F. *A Nation of Immigrants.* Introduction by Robert Kennedy. New York: Harper & Row, Publishers, 1964.

Laboulaye, Edouard de. *Histoire des Etats-Unis.* 3 vols. Paris: 1855.

_____[pseud. Docteur René Lefebvre]. *Paris en Amérique.* Paris: Charpentier, 1863, reissued 1879.

Lanoux, Armand. *1900, La Bourgeoisie absolue...Amours 1900.* Paris: Hachette, 1961, reissued 1973.

Levine, Benjamin, and Isabelle F. Story. *Statue of Liberty, National Monument, Liberty's Island, New York.* U.S. National Park Service, 1952, reissued 1961.

Pauli, Hertha Ernestine. *Gateway to America: Miss Liberty's First Hundred Years.* Illustrated by Leonard Voshburgh. New York: 1965.

_____and E. B. Ashton. *I Lift My Lamp: The Way of the Symbol.* New York: Appleton Century Crofts, 1948.

Top:

In the Luxembourg Gardens. A sculpture of the Lady offered by Bartholdi to the city of Paris.

In Poitiers. A postcard of the sculpture that once stood in that city. *Collection France Debuisson, Paris.*

Price, Willadene. *Bartholdi and the Statue of Liberty.* Chicago: Rand, McNally and Co., 1959, reissued 1973.

Roz, Firmin. *Histoire des Etats-Unis.* Paris: Arthème Fayard et Cie, 1930.

Seitz, Don C. *Joseph Pulitzer, His Life and Letters.* New York: Simon & Schuster, 1924.

Stoddard, Seneca Ray. *Statue of Liberty Enlightening the World Photographed...by S. R. Stoddard.* Glens Falls, N.Y.: S. R. Stoddard, 1891.

Stone, Ross Conway. *A Way to See and Study the Statue of Liberty Enlightening the World.* New York: Bullion Pub. Co., 1887.

Swanberg, W. A. *Pulitzer.* New York: Charles Scribner's Sons, 1967.

Trachtenberg, Marvin. *The Statue of Liberty.* London: Penquin Books, 1977.

Weimbaum, Paul. *Statue of Liberty: Heritage of America.* K. C. Publications, reissued 1980.

Williams, Archibald. *Engineering Wonders of the World.* Vol. 3. London and New York: Thomas Nelson and Sons, n.d.

Articles

Betz, Jacques. "Dans le sillage de Bartholdi." *Annuaire de Colmar,* 1954.

Blanc, Charles. "De la conception dans les oeuvres d'art, à propos du procès de M. Bartholdi, statuaire, contre la ville de Marseille." *Le Temps,* 1865.

————— *Le Temps,* March 27, 1878.

Boistel, J. de. "La Statue de la Liberté." In "Les Documents maçonniques." *Vichy,* no. 2, November 1942.

De Kay, Charles. "France to America." *Scribner's Monthly Illustrated Magazine,* vol. XIV, June 1877

Laboulaye, André de. "La Statue de la Liberté, 1886–1936." *The Franco-American Review,* vol. II, 1938.

Laboulaye, Edouard de. "La Statue de la Liberté." Unedited letter from Edouard de Laboulaye to Miss Mary Booth. *The French-American Review,* vol. II, no. 4 (1949).

Lantoine, Albert. "Bartholdi et la Franc-maçonnerie." *Le Symbolisme,* no. 245.

Riols, Jacques. "La Statue de la Liberté." *Pétrole Progrès,* no. 6 (April 1951).

Rosenberg, Harold. Mère des Exilés. *Dialogue,* vol. VIII, no. 3 (1977).

Seitz, Don C. "She's Still a Thriller: From the People of France." *The Rotarian,* May 1949.

Talansier, Charles. "La Statue de la Liberté Eclairant le Monde." *Le Génie Civil,* vol. III, no. 19 (August 1, 1883).

Trachtenberg, Marvin. "The Statue of Liberty: Transparent Banality or Avant-garde Conundrum." *Art in America,* no. 3 (May–June 1974).

"Bartholdi." *Annuaire de la Société d'Histoire et d'Archéologie de Colmar.* Colmar, 1979.

"Body of Iron, Soul of Fire: A Gift for a Great Lady." *Going Places* (American Express), Sept.–Oct. 1974.

"Liberty Enlightening the World." *Scientific American,* June 13, 1885.

Miscellaneous

• *A propos de l'oeuvre de Gustave Eiffel. Documentation et réflexions sur les circonstances et les méthodes de la construction métallique au XIXe siècle.* Paris: Ministère de la Culture et de l'Environnement, Direction de l'Architecture, Secrétariat à la Recherche architecturale, n.d.

• *An Appeal to the People of the United States on Behalf of the Great Statue, Liberty Enlightening the World. New York Evening Post,* 1882.

- *Bartholdi Souvenir: Liberty Enlightening the World, a Tribute of Respect and Esteem from the French People to the People of the United States*. New York: A. Farrand and Alexander, 1886.
- *Etablissements Gaget-Gauthier et Cie.* Paris: 1880.
- *Etablissements Miège et Buhler.* (One thousand drawings produced for the centenary of the house.) Paris: 1972.
- *Inauguration of the Statue of Liberty Enlightening the World by the President of the United States, on Bedloe's Island, New York, Thursday, October 28, 1886*. New York: D. Appleton and Co., 1887.
- *The Lady in the Harbor.* Catalogue, Bicentennial Exhibition. New York: Statue of Liberty National Monument, May–September 1976.
- *Liberty in Posters, 1917-1978*. Catalogue, Exposition. New York: Statue of Liberty National Monument, National Park Service, 1978.
- *Naissance de la statue de la Liberté: Hommage à Bartholdi*. Catalogue of Exposition, Mairie du XVII ardt., Sept. 23–Oct. 27, 1978.
- *Statue of Liberty Enlightening the World, 1886.* New York: National Statue of Liberty Anniversary Committee, 1936
- *Souvenir Program of the Unveiling and Presentation to the Government of the United States of the Bartholdi Statue of Liberty at Liberty's Island, N.Y. Bay, on Thursday, October 28, 1886.* New York: 1886.
- *La Statue de la Liberté éclairant le Monde: Compt-rendu des conférences faites par A. Bartholdi le 13 novembre 1884 et le 10 mars 1887.* Paris: Imprimerie de Hugonis: janvier 1891.
- *The Statue of Liberty.* Ambassade de France à Washington, Service de presse et d'information, Réf. HS 149.
- *Statue of Liberty National Monument.* Landmark Preservation Commission, no. 1, LP 0931, September 1976.
- *The Statue of Liberty, Its Conception, Its Construction, Its Inauguration*. Official Program. New York: John J. Garnett, 1886.
- *Transactions of the Grand Lodge of Free and Accepted Masons of the State of New York*, New York: 1884. Reissued by the 10th Manhattan Masonic District, 1976.
- *The Statue of Liberty National Monument, Bedloe's Island*. Washington, D.C.: United States National Park Service, 1936.

Top:

In New York City. A version of the statue erected in 1901 crowns the Liberty Warehouse, on West Sixty-fourth Street.

In Saint-Cyr-sur-Mer. The statue stands atop a fountain. The date inscribed on the book is July 14, 1789.

A C K N O W L E D G M E N T S

Our sincere appreciation goes to the duke of Castries, of the Académie Française, and to François de Laboulaye, ambassador of France, co-presidents of the official Franco-American Committee for the Centennial of the Statue of Liberty, for their support, confidence, and assistance.

We would also like to express our gratitude to André Castelot for the warm encouragement that he gave us from the beginning of our enterprise and for his helpful advice.

Our special thanks also to Odile Vaillant and to Jean-Claude Planchet, whose enthusiasm, competence, and friendly cooperation at all times made it possible for this book to be written.

For their goodwill and encouragement, we would like to thank Wilton S. Dillon, director of the office of Smithsonian Symposia and Seminars, in Washington; Alan Fern, director of the National Portrait Gallery, in Washington; Garnet Chapin of the National Park Service, United States Department of the Interior, in Washington; Edward L. Kallop of the National Park Service in Boston; Maurice Agulhon, professor of contemporary history at the University of Paris, Pantheon-Sorbonne, Philippe Lecomte du Nouy, president of the central committee of French societies of New York.

For their advice and patience as well as access to their archives we would like to thank David Moffitt, superintendant of the Statue of Liberty National Monument, in New York; Paul J. Kinney, curator of the museum, and Harvey T. Dixon, librarian; Paul McAdam, director of the American Library in Paris; Pierre Burger, curator of the Bartholdi Museum, in Colmar; Professor Andre Didier, director of the Musée National des Techniques, in Paris; the director and the librarians of the Consérvatoire National des Arts et Métiers, in Paris; Fréderique Devergnes, responsible for the documentation service at the Musée National des Techniques, in Paris; Anne-Claude Lelieur, curator of the Bibliothèque Forney, in Paris; and Michel Devergne, former president of Etablissements Miège et Buhler, in Paris.

For their assistance, their collaboration, and their advice on specific points in the preparation of this book, we would like to thank Flory Barnett, Mark Browne, Alan Naftalis, Carolyn Penrose, Paul Spradling, Hélène Bertini, Marie-Christine Gauthier, Xavier Lay, Daniel Mercheron, Annie Sisombat, Pierre Schwaertzig, Jean Weiler, and our family and friends for their support and participation.

Our appreciation also to those who kindly authorized the reproduction of their works: artists Jean Ainak, Jean Alessandrini, Brennan, Pol Bury, David Byrd, Thibault de Champrosay, Alain Dall'oste, Jean Decaris, Michel Dubré, Erro, Pierre Etaix, Jacques Faizant, Catherine Folatre, Jean-Michel Folon, François Halard, Gotlib, Robert Grossman, Michel Guiré-Vaka, Luis Jiminez, Jean Kapera, Jean Lagarrigue, Roy Lichtenstein, Ludovico de Luigi, Peter Max, Yves Méry, Fr. Mettes, Marta Minujin, Haruo Miyauchi, Jacques Monory, Mordillo, Julia Noonan, Evelyne Noviant, Klaes Oldenburg, Suzanne Osterweil, Piem, Prorokov, Michael Rock, Cosimo Scianna, Eric Seldman, Sine, Neal Slavin, Jean-Claude Suarès, the group Supertramp, Andy Warhol, and Doug Webb.

Collectors: Pierre Beres, Jean Carlu, Ernest L. Chambre, Rodolphe Coigny, Tony Curtis, France Debuisson, Alexina Duchamp, Ralph O. Esmerian, Nicole Ferraci, Alain Fildier, Katharine D. Hellman, Christophe L., Michel de Laboulaye, Norman and Frances Lear, Dr. Erich Marx, Mertha Mole, Joseph Pulitzer, Jr., Richard Ravitz, Pierre Restancy, Samuel Rosenberg, and Gilbert Salachas.

Museums, libraries, and associations: American Library in Paris; the Boy Scouts of America, Irving, Texas; the Cooper-Hewitt Museum—the Smithsonian Institution's National Museum of Design, New York; the Free French Press and Information Service, New York; the Greater New York Conference on Soviet Jewry, New York; the Library of Congress, Washington; the Museum of American Folk Art, New York; the Museum of the City of New York; the Museum of Modern Art, New York; the National Archives, Washington; the New York Public Library, New York; the New York Public Library at Lincoln Center, New York; Public Collection of Fine Arts, Print Room, Basel; the Statue of Liberty National Monument, National Park Service, New York; the Trustees of Columbia University, New York; the Bibliothèque Forney, Paris; the Ecole Nationale Superieure des Beaux Arts, Paris; the Zabriskie Gallery, Paris; the Grand Orient de France, Paris; the Monnaie de Paris, Paris; the Institut National de la Propriété industrielle, Paris; the Musée Bartholdi and the city of Colmar; the Musée Carnavalet, Paris; the Musée National des Techniques and the Bibliothèque du Conservatoire National des Arts et Métiers, Paris; the Musée de la Coopération Franco-Americaine, Blérancourt; the Louvre, Paris; and the Musée de la Poste, Paris.

Societies and agencies: A & M Records Europe S.A.; APEI Press Agency, Paris; Brown and Williamson Tobacco Corporation, Brussels; Christiane Charillon, Paris; Emigrant Savings Bank, New York; FFCM, Paris; Fluide Glacial, Paris; G.M.C. Ayer, Paris; Gaumont International, Paris; Hill Studio, Clinton, Iowa; Holland America Line, Rotterdam; Impact F.C.B. Paris; LePoint, Paris; Loïs France, Paris; Etablissements Miège et Buhler, Paris; National Broadcasting Company, Inc., New York; Pan Am, Paris; the Peace Corps, Washington; Radio City Music Hall Productions, Inc., New York; S.N.C.F., Paris; Agency Taurus, Paris; The *Times* of London; Twentieth Century Fox Film, Inc., Continental Division, Paris Office; Cinémas Utopia, Valencia, Verveine du Velay, Le Puy en Velay, Yang Films, Paris; Young and Rubicam Agency, New York; Young Men's Christian Association, Chicago.

Italicized page numbers indicate that indexed entries on those pages fall within captions.

A

Adam, P. *73*
Ainak, Jean *174*
Alessandrini, Jean *161*
American Committee for the Statue of Liberty 62, 77–78, 80, 81, 84, 100
American Electric Company 100
American Museum of Immigration *141*, 146, 148
American Scenic and Historic Preservation Society 146
Ayer, G.M.C. *174*

B

Baheux de Puysieux, Jeanne-Emilie (Mme. Bartholdi) 48, *48*, 62
Bartholdi, Frédéric Auguste 8, 91, 107, 116, 120, 126, 138, 151, *174*, and armature for Liberty 68, 71, artistic conservatism of 17, 19, 22–23, 30, 153, background of 19, 22, and colossal sculpture 9, 22–26, copyright of Liberty 168, *171*, death of 132, in Egypt 22–23, design for Liberty 40–41, 44, and design for pedestal 77–78, and Franco-Prussian War 32–33, and Freemasonry 44, honorary citizenship for *101*, and human models for Liberty 48, impression of New York Harbor 36, Lafayette, statue of *47*, 58, 62, and lighting system of Liberty 100, *Lion of Belfort* 22, 30, *30*, marries 62, mother of 48, original drawings for Liberty 36, *36, 38, 44*, and origins for idea of Liberty 16, 17, and Philadelphia Exposition 54–55, plaster model of Liberty *53*, 54–55, *56*, prepares bust of Liberty for exhibition 68, project for Ismail Pasha 23–24, selects assistants for Liberty project 48, studio of *41*, and symbolism of Liberty 44, 47, Tiffany globe for 91, *93*, and unveiling of Liberty 9, 98, *Vercingétorix 46*, visits U.S. for groundwork of project 7, 33, 36, 40, 55, 58, 62, watercolors by *33*
Bartholdi, Philippe 51
Bastedo, Capt. Paul *140*
Bavaria (Munich) 32
Bedloe, Isaac 77
Bedloe's Island 8, 36, 52, *52*, 58, 62, 74, 77, 91, 98, 107, 111, 145–46
Berlin, Irving 118, 142, 144, *146*, 154
Bigot, Charles 98
Bland, Richard 92
Boorstin, Daniel J. 9
Borglum, Gutzon *130*, 138, *150*
Boring and Tilton 111
Brennan *158*
Brenner, Jean *48*
Breton, André *178*
Brooklyn Bridge 7, 9, 24, *24*
Bruat, Adm. Jean 22
Bryan, William Jennings 104, 106–107, *111*
Bryant, William Cullen 62
Bury, Pol *174*
Butler, Richard 62, 80, 85

C

Cabet, M. *26*
Calendar of Liberty *134*
Canova, Antonio *40, 47*
Caricatures of Liberty *42, 158–65,* 159
Carlu, Natacha *154*
Castoria 146
Chain of Union, The 44, *45,* 47
Chapu, M. *26*
Chares of Lindos 32
Circle Line ferry service 148
Civil War American 13–14, 16
Cleveland, Grover 9, 84, 92, 94, *96,* 98, 103–104, 106, 116, 120
Clock image of Liberty *134*
Colossal sculpture 9, 22–26, 30, 32, *32, 33,* 47–48, 117
Colossus of Rhodes 30, *32,* 117
Columbia, female figure of *36, 42,* 126
Congress, American 92, *96,* 132, 125, 144
Conterno, G.E. *106*
Corsi, Edward 113–14, 146
Cosimo *161*
Crawford, Thomas 32, 44
Crespi, G.B. *28, 32,* 47, 68

D

Dargaud, Victor *73*
Debs, Eugene V. 106, 107
Deinocrates *33*
Delacroix, Eugène *20,* 30, 44
de Lesseps, Ferdinand 24, 25, 52, 71, 73, 94
Depew, Chauncey M. 98, 104, 116, 139
Despont, Thierry *148*
Dubré, Michel *172*
Duchamp, Marcel *178*
Duplessis-Beteaux *20*
Du Pont, Pierre S., III 146

E

Eiffel, Gustave 8, 9, 25, 120, 132, and armature for Liberty 48, *62,* 68, 71, Garabit bridge *22,* 24, Eiffel Tower 9, 68
Ellis, Samuel 111
Ellis Island 8, 110–11, 113, *116, 117,* 125, 144, 146, 148
Empire State Building 9, 139
Etex, Antoine 22
Evarts, William M. 62, 77, 85, 103, 116, 117, 146
Evening Telegram, New York *78, 122*

F

Faizant, Jacques *164, 165*
Fede, Pio *40*
Ferries to Liberty Island 148
Fischer, Carl *158*
Flattau, William 132
Folon *161*
Foran Act 110
Forney, John W. 51, 52
Fort Wood, Bedloe's Island 77, 81,

130, 132, 139
Franco-American relations 8, 13–14, 16, 58, 126, 139, 142, 153
Franco-American Union 51–52, *51,* 55, 62, 68, 71, 80
Franco-American-Statue of Liberty-New York Committee 62
Franco-Prussian War 8, 13–14, 16, 32–33
Franklin, Benjamin 14, *16, 42*
Free Mason, The 44
Freemasonry 44, *45,* 47, 84–85
French-American Committee for the Restoration of the Statue of Liberty 148
French Revolution 41, 44
French Third Republic 14, 33, 40, 73

G

Gaget, Emile 48
Gaget, Gauthier and Company 8, 13, 48 *56, 68, 70,* 71, 73
Garland, Attorney General Augustus 120
George, Henry 106, 107
Germany 14, 110, 120, 125, 126
Gibson, Charles Dana *122*
Godwin, Parke 62
Goldberg, Rube 139
Gompers, Samuel 123
Gounod, Charles *54,* 55, *55*
Governor's Island 77
Grant, Madison *122*
Grant, Ulysses S. *24,* 36, 52, 62, 68, 94, letter to *52*
Grévy, Francois *70*
Guiré-Vaka, Michel *163*

H

Haggerty, Mick *177*
Hampson, E.P., and Company 100
Handkerchief image of Liberty *133*
Harmony Club 52, 62, 98
Harte, Bret 117
Herald, New York 58, 129–30, 132
Hewitt, Abram S. 62, 92, 106
Hine, Lewis Wickes *115*
Holland-America Line *169*
Horgan, Paul 9
Horenz, Emile *107*
Hugo, Victor 9, 13
Hungarian revolt (1956) 145
Hunt, Richard Morris 9, 80, *82,* 85, 91, 111

I

Iacocca, Lee J. 148
Immigration, American 8–9, 13, 107–11, 113–14, *114,* 116–18, *118,* 120, *120,* 122–123, *122,* 125–26, causes of 108–10, closing the doors 120, 122–23, 125, linked to Liberty 120, museum on *141,* 146, 148, numbers 110, post-WWII *141,* 144, processing procedure 113, *116, 117,* quota system 123, 125, racism and prejudice in 120, 122–23

Ingraham, E. and Company *134*
Iran Air *174*
Isère (ship of war) *73, 74, 74, 75,* 77
Ismail Pasha 23–24, 80

J

Janet-Lange, A.L. *20*
Jefferson, Thomas 14
Johnson, Lyndon B. 125
Johnson-Read Act of 1924 123, 125
Judge *94*
Jusserand, Jules 139

K

Kennedy, John F. 125
Kent Cigarettes *172*
Khomeini, Ayatollah 159, *164*
Krokodil 158

L

Labor, immigration and 110, 120, *120,* 122–23, 125
Laboulaye, André de 142
Laboulaye, Edouard-René Lefebvre de 9, 14–16, *16,* 23, 33, 36, 44, 47, 103, 116, 120, 146, and administration of project 51–52
Lafayette, Marquis de 14, 22, 44, *47,* 51, 58, 62, 78
Lagarrigue, Jean *161, 162*
LaGuardia, Fiorello 142
Laval, Mlle. Josie 139
Law, Ruth 139
Lawrence, Franck R. 85
Lazarus, Emma 8, 116–18, *118,* 120, 125, 126, 151, "The New Colossus" 117–18 (text) *118, 119,* 125, 126
League of Nations 125, 126
Lebrun, René 142
LeFaivre, Albert 98
Leslie's 78
Leyendecker, J.C. *152*
Libertas Americana *16, 42*
Liberation of the Blacks, The 47
Liberty Bonds *124,* 126, *126, 152*
Liberty Enlightening the World *see* Statue of Liberty
Liberty Island 145–46, *see also* Bedloe's Island
Liberty Moving and Storage Company 132
Lichtenstein, Roy *174, 177*
Life 78
Lighthouse Board, Dept. of Treasury 91, 100, 130, 132
Lighthouses, monumental *28*
Lincoln, Abraham 16
Loïs jeans *172*
Longfellow, Henry Wadsworth 36
Lowell, James Russell 118

M

MacMahon, Marshal 52
Mahood *164*
Mamikonian, Helen 8–9
Martin, Henri 44, 71
Marx Brothers *174*
Max, Peter *174*

McCarran-Walter Act 125
McClanahan, Lester 151
McKinley, William 107
Meany, George 146
Méry, Yves 175
Mettes 169
Millard, Harrison 106
Minujin, Marta 178
Miss Liberty (Berlin/Sherwood) 142, 144, 146, 154
Miyauchi, Haruo 161
Monumental sculpture see Colossal sculpture
Monuments, tallest, of world 28
Moran, Edward 98, 154
Mordillo 165
Morgan, Edwin D. 62
Morice Brothers 26
Morton, Levi P. 64, 69, 71, 73
Mott, J. L. Ironworks 134
Mount Rushmore memorial 130, 138
Mouvement Scientifique, Le 105
Musical Solemnity 54, 55

N

Napoleon III 8, 14, 16, 33, 40
Nast, Thomas 19, 78, 100, 120, 122
National Park Service 132, 142, 146, 148
New Colossus, The (Lazarus) 118, 119, 125, 126, text of 117-18
New Deal 142
New Orleans 1885 Exposition 108
New York City 104, funding for Liberty project 58, 62, national antipathy toward 78
New York 1904 174
New York Times, The 58
Nixon, Richard M. 146
Noviant, Eveleyne 173

O

Osterweil, Suzanne 177

P

Paine, Thomas 110
Pan Am ad 174
Paris Universal Exposition of 1878 25, 60, 61, 68
Paus, Herbert 154
Peace Corps poster 158
Pedestal of Liberty 7, 9, Bartholdi drawing for 38, casting of 129, completion of 86, 91, design for 77-78, 80, 82, 85, 87, elevator in 86, 87, 132, 139, funding of 55, 58, 62, 74, 78, 78, 80, 80, 81, 81, 84, 85, 85, 86, 88, 90-91, laying of foundation 80-81, 84-85, 84, 87,
Pezzicar 19
Phidias 30

Philadelphia 62, Centennial Exposition of 1876 19, 24, 36, 51, 54-55, 58, 58
Phrygian cap 41, 42, 44, 47
Piem 164
Pilcher, Mrs. Theodore 133
Planet of the Apes 162
Point, Le 173
Postcards of Liberty 134
Poster art of Liberty 62, 124, 126, 126, 152, 158, 169
Potter, Rev. Henry C. 98
Propaganda: art as 30, use of Liberty in 145-46, 158-65. See also Liberty Bonds
Puck 112
Pulitzer, Joseph 9, 74, 85, 85, 88, 90, 93, 94, 120, 129, 134, 138, 151, 168
Pulitzer, Ralph 138, 139

R

Rapp, Gen. Jean 22
Renaud, Sophie 107
Repoussé technique 47-48, 65
Robbins, Jerome 146
Robert, Elias 44
Rochambeau, Gen. Jean-Baptiste de 14, 51
Roebling, John 25
Roebling, Washington 25
Roger, L. 20
Roosevelt, Franklin D. 120, 140, 142
Roosevelt, Theodore 7, 104, 106, 132
Rosenberg, Harold 153

S

Salmon, Adolf 52-53
Sargent, John Singer 85
Satiric use of Liberty 42, 158-65, 159
Schaffner, Franklin J. 162
Scheffer, Ary 19, 22, 48
Schilling, J.: Germania 26, 32
Schuyler, Georgina 118
Sculpture, colossal see Colossal sculpture
Seldman, Eric 175
Sherman, William Tecumseh 77
Sherwood, Robert E. 142, 146
Singer, Mrs. Isaac Merrit 48
Skouras, Spyros 146
Social change in 19th Century America 103-104, 106-10
Soitoux, Jean-François 22
Spanish-American War 107
Stamps, Liberty image on 154, 154, 156
Statue of Liberty ("Liberty Enlightening the World"): administration of project 51-52, adopted as symbol of liberty and U.S. 125-26, 124, 126, American indifference to project 78,

80, armature of 48, 62, 65, 68, 71, 80, Army as custodian of 130, 132, 142, 144, arrives in N.Y. 74, 75, 77, assembly in N.Y. 86, 91, assembly in Paris 68, canvas backdrop curtain of 54, 55, 58 caricatures of 158-65, 159, ceremony proffering to American people 69, 73-74, commercial advertising and 146, 168, 168-75, conservation history and problems, 129-30, 132, 137-39, 142, 144-46, 148-49, 151, copper for 48, 51, 61, 65, copyright of image 168, 171, design of 40-41, 44, dimensions and weight of 7, driving of first rivet 64, eightieth anniversary 151, emotional appeal of 129, fiftieth anniversary 140, 142, foot of 70, funding of 8, 51-52, 54-55, 58, 62, 68, 71, 92, graffiti on 130, 138, head of 60, 61, 68, 88, 96, headdress, selection of 47, human models for features of 48, 48, ideological influences on project 44, 47, immigrant responses to 113-14, as inspiration to artists 154-78, 174, as lighthouse 91, 100, 132, lighting system of 100, 100, 130, 131, 137-39, linked to immigration 120, lottery for funding 71, medium, selection of 47-48, miniatures of 129, 134, models for 41-44, 47, museum at 141, 146, 148, music in celebration of 54, 55, 55, 106, 107, as national monument 132, 148, "The New Colossus" (Lazarus) 117-18, 118, 119, 125, 126, 1916 renovation of 130, 132, 137, 1931 renovation of 139, 1938 renovation of 136, 137, 1980s renovation of 148-49, 148-51, 151, operating budget of 148, origin of idea for 16-17, 19, placement of, importance of 7, plaster model of 54-55, 56, political demonstrations at 146, propaganda uses of 126, 145-46, 158-65, 159, replica of 132, repoussé technique 47-48, 65, subscription for 58, 62, 68, symbolism of 8, 9, 13-14, 44, 47, 124, 125-26, 126, 154, 159, 168, as tourist attraction, 130, 132, 139, 148, transporting of 73-74, 73-74, unveiling of, 90, 92, 94, 94, 96, 98, 100, as work of art 153, WPA work on 142. See also Pedestal of Liberty, Torch and hand of Liberty.
Statue of Liberty-Ellis Island Foundation 148
Statue of Liberty National Monument 148
Stieglitz, Alfred 114
Stone, Gen. Charles Pomeroy 80, 81, 85, 91, 92, 94, 98
Storrs, Rev. Richard 98
Suarès, Jean-Claude 161
Suez Canal 24, 33, 52
Sumner, Charles 36
Sun's rays, symbolism of 47

Supertramp 177

T

Technological innovation in the nineteenth century 24-25, 103-104
Tiffany globe 91, 93
Tilton, Edward 111
Tocqueville, Alexis de 14, 51, 103
Torch and hand of Liberty 56, 58, 139, closed to public 132, 137, creation of 54-55, 58, 58, lighting system, 100, 101, 130, 131, 137-39, in Madison Square 68, renovation of 130, 131, 137-39, 148
Trachtenberg, Marvin 153
Truman, Harry S. 8
Twain, Mark 117

U

Uncle Sam symbol 125-26
United States: anti-Americanism 159, propaganda use of Liberty 126, social and political change in, during 19th century 103-104, 106-10, 109-11, urban development 103-104, 106. See also Immigration.

V

Varni, Santo 40
Vietnam Veterans Against the War 146
Viollet-le-Duc, Eugène 48, 52, 68

W

War Department 100, 130, 132
War Food Administration 126
Warhol, Andy 174, 178
War Savings Certificates 126
War Savings Stamps 126, 154
Washburne, Elihu 51, 52, 55
Washington Monument 8, 32
Watch pocket, image of Liberty 134
Weathervane image of Liberty 134
Webb, Doug 175
Weiss, Arnold 114
West, Mae 174
White, Mrs. Glenn C. 151
Whitman, Walt 117
Wilson, Woodrow 120, 125, 126, 139
Windom, William 120
Window, stained-glass, of Liberty 134
WNBC Radio 172
Woolworth Building 104
Wonders of the world 26, 30
Works Progress Administration (WPA) 142
World New York 85, 88, 90, 94, 98, 109, 134, 138
World War I 123, 125-26
World War II 142
Wright, Brothers 129, 134, 139, 168